MULTICULTURAL EDUCATION SERIES

James A. Banks, Series Editor

BEYOND THE BIG HOUSE

African American Educators on Teacher Education

GLORIA LADSON-BILLINGS

TEACHERS COLLEGE PRESS

Teachers College
Columbia University
New York and London

For Kevin,
who taught me to parent with integrity.

Published by Teachers College Press, 1234 Amsterdam Avenue, New York, NY 10027

Chapter opening photographs: Georgia State University (*Joyce King*); Michael T. Steibel (*Carl Grant*); Wolf Camera (*Jacqueline Jordan Irvine*); Images by Edy (*Geneva Gay*); Washington University (*William Tate*); Marc Studer, UW Bothell Campus Media Center (*Cherry A. McGee Banks*); Michael Upright (*Lisa Delpit*)

Portions of Chapter 1 were adapted from an earlier work (Ladson-Billings, 2002).
Portions of Chapter 2 were adapted from an earlier work (Ladson-Billings, 2003).

Library of Congress Cataloging-in-Publication Data

Ladson-Billings, Gloria, 1947–
    Beyond the big house : African American educators on teacher education / Gloria Ladson-Billings
        p. cm. – (Multicultural education series)
    Includes bibliographical references (p.) and index.
    ISBN 0-8077-4582-0 (cloth : alk. paper) – ISBN 0-8077-4581-2 (pbk. : alk. paper)
        1. African American teachers – Training of. 2. African American teachers – Attitudes.
    3. Teacher educators – United States – Attitudes. 4. Teachers colleges – United States –
    Faculty. I. Title. II. Multicultural education series (New York, N.Y.)

LC2782.L33 2005
371.1'0089'960–dc22

2005041709

ISBN 0-8077-4581-2 (paper)
ISBN 0-8077-4582-0 (cloth)

Printed on acid-free paper

Manufactured in the United States of America

12 11 10 09 08 07 06 05   8 7 6 5 4 3 2 1

Contents

Series Foreword

The nation's deepening ethnic texture, interracial tension and conflict, and the increasing percentage of students who speak a first language other than English make multicultural education imperative in the 21st century. The U.S. Census Bureau (2000) estimated that people of color made up 28% of the nation's population in 2000 and predicted that they would make up 38% in 2025 and 47% in 2050. In March 2004, the Census revised its projections and predicted that by 2050 people of color and Whites would each make up 50% of the U.S. population (El Nasser, 2004).

American classrooms are experiencing the largest influx of immigrant students since the beginning of the 20th century. About a million immigrants are making the United States their home each year (Martin & Midgley, 1999). More than 7.5 million legal immigrants settled in the United States between 1991 and 1998, most of whom came from nations in Latin America and Asia (Riche, 2000). A large but undetermined number of undocumented immigrants also enter the United States each year. The influence of an increasingly ethnically diverse population on the nation's schools, colleges, and universities is and will continue to be enormous.

Forty percent of the students enrolled in the nation's schools in 2001 were students of color. This percentage is increasing each year, primarily because of the growth in the percentage of Latino students (Martinez & Curry, 1999). In some of the nation's largest cities and metropolitan areas, such as Chicago, Los Angeles, Washington, DC, New York, Seattle, and San Francisco, half or more of the public school students are students of color. During the 1998–1999 school year, students of color made up 63.1% of the student population in the public schools of California, the nation's largest state (California State Department of Education, 2000).

Language and religious diversity is also increasing among the nation's student population. In 2000, about 20% of the school-age population spoke a language at home other than English (U.S. Census Bureau, 2000). Harvard professor Diana L. Eck (2001) calls the United States the "most religiously diverse nation on earth" (p. 4). Most teachers now in the classroom and in teacher education programs are likely to have students from diverse ethnic, racial, language, and religious groups in their classrooms during their careers. This is true for both inner-city and suburban teachers.

An important goal of multicultural education is to improve race relations and to help all students acquire the knowledge, attitudes, and skills needed to participate in cross-cultural interactions and in personal, social, and civic action that will help make our nation more democratic and just. Multicultural education is consequently as important for middle-class White suburban students as it is for students of color who live in the inner city. Multicultural education fosters the public good and the overarching goals of the commonwealth.

The major purpose of the *Multicultural Education Series* is to provide preservice educators, practicing educators, graduate students, scholars, and policy makers with an interrelated and comprehensive set of books that summarizes and analyzes important research, theory, and practice related to the education of ethnic, racial, cultural, and language groups in the United States and the education of mainstream students about diversity. The books in the *Series* provide research, theoretical, and practical knowledge about the behaviors and learning characteristics of students of color, language minority students, and low-income students. They also provide knowledge about ways to improve academic achievement and race relations in educational settings.

The definition of multicultural education in the *Handbook of Research on Multicultural Education* (Banks & Banks, 2004) is used in the *Series*: Multicultural education is "*a field of study designed to increase educational equity for all students that incorporates, for this purpose, content, concepts, principles, theories, and paradigms from history, the social and behavioral sciences, and particularly from ethnic studies and women's studies*" (p. xii). In the *Series*, as in the *Handbook*, multicultural education is considered a "metadiscipline."

The dimensions of multicultural education, developed by Banks (2004) and described in the *Handbook of Research on Multicultural Education*, provide the conceptual framework for the development of the books in the *Series*. They are *content integration, the knowledge construction process, prejudice reduction, an equity pedagogy,* and *an empowering school culture and social structure.* To implement multicultural education effectively, teachers and administrators must attend to each of the five dimensions of multicultural education. They should use content from diverse groups when teaching concepts and skills, help students to understand how knowledge in the various disciplines is constructed, help students to develop positive intergroup attitudes and behaviors, and modify their teaching strategies so that students from different racial, cultural, language, and social-class groups will experience equal educational opportunities. The total environment and culture of the school must also be transformed so that students from diverse groups will experience equal status in the culture and life of the school.

Although the five dimensions of multicultural education are highly interrelated, each requires deliberate attention and focus. Each book in the series focuses on one or more of the dimensions, although each book deals with all of them to some extent because of the highly interrelated characteristics of the dimensions.

As Ladson-Billings points out in this informative and engaging book, no group is less studied than teacher educators. Researchers in education—like researchers in other fields and disciplines—usually study "others"—people unlike themselves—or their students. African American teacher educators have been nearly invisible in the literature prior to the publication of this pioneering and innovative book.

In this beautifully crafted and richly textured book, Ladson-Billings describes the lives, struggles, hopes, dreams, and triumphs of seven African American teacher educators who have made substantial contributions to teaching, service, and research. By identifying a figure in African American history to which she compares each educator, Ladson-Billings not only deepens the reader's knowledge of Black history but also shows how the struggle for freedom by African Americans crosses generations. The issues and people have varied in different historical periods but the struggle for freedom and social justice has been consistent in the Black experience since Africans were forced to come to America in chains beginning in the 17th century.

Ladson-Billings uses a powerful and complex metaphor—the Big House—to describe the barriers to reform that these African American teacher educators experience in the predominantly White institutions in which they work. The Big House metaphor is also used to describe the ways in which these educators have creatively worked to overcome barriers and to bring about institutional change. The Big House was the mansion on large plantations in which the owner and his family lived. The enslaved people who worked in the Big House had a higher status than field workers. However, their fate was tightly connected to the fate of the field-workers, just as the destiny of African American teacher educators is tied to the condition of African American students.

Ladson-Billings uses the Big House metaphor to describe how departments, schools, and colleges of education reflect institutional values that support the status quo and impede the academic achievement and social growth of African American students and students from other marginalized groups. Consequently, African American teacher educators in predominantly White colleges and universities are "outsiders within" (Collins, 2000) who seek to reform teacher education programs in substantial ways in order to advance educational equality.

In telling the stories of seven teacher educators, Ladson-Billings discloses information about her own journey, commitments, and work to reform teacher education. Her personal and professional relationships with these seven teacher educators gave Ladson-Billings a unique opportunity to hear their life stories. They trusted and respected her as a friend and researcher and consequently freely shared their beliefs, values, and life stories, which greatly enrich this book.

Crosscutting themes in this book reveal how the worlds of the seven teacher educators are connected. Each is the only African American or one of several within her or his department, school, or college and consequently travels a lonely road. Each has a strong commitment to social justice and equality and has—through teaching, research, and service—tried to advance social justice work in the institutions in which she or he works. Each is also involved in a struggle to engage White colleagues and students in reforms that will result in greater educational equality for all students.

The teacher educators described in this book are highly successful individuals who have experienced success and triumphs despite having faced tremendous obstacles. Their success in elementary school, high school, and college—and in their careers—resulted from their commitment, vision, hard work, and the support of their families and the African American community.

This book contains important lessons about how hope, commitment, tenacity, and hard work can triumph over great odds. The life stories in it epitomize Mary McLeod Bethune's (n.d.) belief that "Faith is the first factor in a life devoted to service. Without faith, nothing is possible. With it, nothing is impossible." By uncovering and telling the stories of this group of distinguished and influential teacher educators, Ladson-Billings has made a significant contribution to the profession and to the research literature. I am confident that this creative, visionary, and informative book will have the lasting influence it deserves.

James A. Banks
Series Editor

REFERENCES

Banks, J. A. (Ed.). (1996). *Multicultural education, transformative knowledge, and action: Historical and contemporary perspectives.* New York: Teachers College Press.

Banks, J. A. (2004). Multicultural education: Historical development, dimensions, and practice. In J. A. Banks & C. A. M. Banks (Eds.), *Handbook of research on multicultural education* (2nd ed., pp. 3–29). San Francisco: Jossey-Bass.

Banks, J. A., & Banks, C. A. M. (Eds.). (2004). *Handbook of research on multicultural education* (2nd ed.). San Francisco: Jossey-Bass.

Bethune, M. M. (n.d.). *Dr. Mary McCleod Bethune's last will and testament.* Retrieved July 17, 2004, from http://www.cookman.edu/Welcome/Founder/last_will.htm

California State Department of Education. (2000). Retrieved July 14, 2004, from http://data1.cde.ca.gov/dataquest

Collins, P. H. (2000). *Black feminist thought: Knowledge, consciousness, and the politics of empowerment.* New York: Routledge.

Eck, D. L. (2001). *A new religious America: How a "Christian country" has become the world's most religiously diverse nation.* New York: HarperSanFrancisco.

El Nasser, H. (2004, March 18). Census projects growing diversity: By 2050: Population burst, societal shifts. *USA Today*, p. 1A.

Martin, P., & Midgley, E. (1999). Immigration to the United States. *Population Bulletin*, 54(2), 1–44. Washington, DC: Population Reference Bureau.

Martinez, G. M., & Curry A. E. (1999, September). *Current population reports: School enrollment–social and economic characteristics of students* (update). Washington, DC: U.S. Census Bureau.

Riche, M. F. (2000). America's diversity and growth: Signposts for the 21st century. *Population Bulletin*, 55(2), 1–43. Washington, DC: Population Reference Bureau.

U.S. Census Bureau (2000). *Statistical abstract of the United States* (120th ed.). Washington, DC: U.S. Government Printing Office.

Preface

Most scholars are challenged to do one of two things—research and write about something new, or research and write about something in a new way. In this volume I have attempted to do a bit of both. What's new is a look at the lives of African American teacher educators. The obvious reason for writing about African American teacher educators is to fill the void in the literature. But another reason for writing about African American teacher educators is to explore the unique perspectives they bring to the profession. As members of one of the society's more marginalized groups, how do African Americans fulfill their mandate to prepare teachers to educate subsequent generations of Americans?

Little is written about the lives of teacher educators. Ducharme (1993) focused on this topic in general but had little to say about the experiences of African American teacher educators. In the midst of all the rhetoric about diversity, little attention has been focused on the lack of diversity in the professoriate, particularly in the teacher education professoriate.

However, this volume is not merely about reporting on the lives of African American teacher educators in a conventional way. I do not confine myself to the abysmal statistics and identity politics of today's campuses. Instead I have chosen to recruit the metaphor of slavery's Big House to create a frame for understanding the ambivalent position that African American teacher educators find themselves in as members of the academy. I chose the slavery metaphor because of the way this chapter of our history has been such a defining aspect of all of our lives. Even when we think we are distant from the event in both time and sentiment, language, perspectives, policy, symbols, and feelings emerge that place us back in that place where human worth was rated and ranked on the basis of skin color.

In addition to employing the Big House metaphor I have created portraits of well-known and highly regarded African American teacher educators. In the tradition of Lawrence-Lightfoot and Davis (1997) I have attempted to craft intimate portraits of these teacher educators, and this intimacy is achieved through my own relationship with each of the project participants.

The new thing I have attempted is the use of historical and/or legendary personalities that I have superimposed over each participant's life. Instead of writing a straight narrative text about the participants' biographies, I have searched the rich history and culture of African American experience to find people who might be emblematic of the perspectives and principles of the African American teacher educators who agreed to participate in this project. I chose to work in this way both as an homage to the teacher educators and as an opportunity to educate and inform the reader. Few mainstream curricula or texts have space for the huge pantheon of significant African Americans whose social, cultural, political, scientific, or spiritual efforts made life better for us all.

Doing my work in this way is risky. It stands outside of the traditional canons of research and scholarship. Yet we know that scholarship is advanced not only through replication but also through innovation.

In Chapter 1 I provide an introduction of the project that includes both an explanation for the use of the Big House metaphor and the way such a metaphor serves as an appropriate rubric for understanding the lives and work of African American teacher educators. This chapter gives demographic information about teacher educators and documents the literature void that exists regarding African American teacher educators.

Chapter 2 details the methodological work of the project. The first part of the chapter explores the way teacher education as an institution creates a specific rhetoric that we repeat with every new generation of new teachers. Unfortunately, this rhetoric keeps us from breaking some bad habits and from beginning to do new things to meet the current challenges of teaching. I explain why this rhetoric creates a level of dissonance for African American teacher educators that makes their work more difficult and sometimes less satisfying.

The second part of Chapter 2 focuses on the development of this project and the methodological strategies I used to construct this work. I have foregrounded the method in this volume because I see this methodological move as more than a new way to do narrative scholarship; it is also a new way to ask important epistemological questions about the variety of ways we can come to know another human being. This chapter also raises new questions about subjectivity and positionality of both the researcher and the researched—the knower and the known. Inherent in this work is the question of how researchers handle equal status relationships in the context of their work. Typically, researchers place themselves in positions where they have higher status. Studies of students, parents, teachers, and other school personnel invariably imply that the educational researcher is in the more privileged position, and no matter what terminology the researcher uses to convey an equalization of status, the broader cultural referent of "research-er" bestows more status on the researcher.

In this book I was not only interacting with other researchers; I was interacting with other researchers whose own scholarly profiles equaled or surpassed my own. So luminous is the image of each of the book's par-ticipants that we decided not to follow the traditional research protocol of blinding their identities. It is important that readers have the opportunity to see them as three-dimensional scholars who struggle with some similar challenges related to their racial and cultural affiliations.

Each of the Chapters 3 through 8 includes a narrative by an interview participant. The chapters begin with an introduction of the historical or leg-endary personality I selected and include the relationship I have drawn be-tween the teacher educator and his or her historical or legendary alter ego. I have used this strategy both to introduce a wider audience to some aspects of African American history and culture with which they may be unfamiliar and to create another way to think about the work of African American teacher educators. Each of these characterizations reflects the license I took in the development of the scholarly portraits.

Chapters 3 through 8 also include sections about my relationships with the project participants. Here, in each portrait, I expose my subjectivity and underscore my lack of neutrality in this process. Although I make no claims to artistic greatness, I make these relationships transparent in much the way any knowledgeable art lover can recognize a Rembrandt or a Van Gogh, a Catlett or a Bearden. My presence is not an attempt to garner adulation but rather a way to be more open about the process and my role in it.

Chapter 9 is both the conclusion and "something extra." I entitled it "Lagniappe," the Louisiana French Creole word for an unexpected gift or extra benefit. In this chapter I include a more truncated picture of another renowned African American teacher educator with whom most readers are familiar, Lisa Delpit. Our inability to make the "portrait sitting" work did not preclude my desire to represent her or her willingness to be a part of the project.

The remainder of the final chapter summarizes the meaning of this project. It asks larger epistemological and methodological questions about qualitative work in general and this work in particular. In this chapter I draw on Lincoln and Denzin's (1998) notion of the "fifth moment" (p. 407) and the tensions of trying to do qualitative work between the dichotomous poles of modernity and postmodernity. I put forth an argument about the need for new scholarship conducted and represented in new ways. I try to make sense of struggling with positivism and postpositivism, issues of legitimation, representing multiple voices, blurring the borders between the sacred and the scientific, and understanding the influence of technology—all tension points identified by Lincoln and Denzin (1998).

I am acutely aware that I wrote this volume in the same moment that the nation was commemorating the 50th anniversary of perhaps the most important Supreme Court decision since the founding of the nation, *Brown v. Board of Education* (1954). Many scholars are debating the merits of the decision and its results in the 21st century. Although I, too, have been critical of the limits of *Brown*, I do not diminish its import on that group of African Americans that has moved into the economic middle class. The people who agreed to participate in these interviews are beneficiaries of *Brown*, if not directly, indirectly through the fervor and mobilization of a social movement. They are among the first generation to fully do their work beyond the Big House.

Acknowledgments

It is always dangerous to try to acknowledge all the people who make a project like this possible. One runs the risk of overlooking some significant person without whom such an undertaking could not happen. However, acknowledgments, no matter how flawed, are always in order. The most obvious people to thank are the project participants—Cherry McGee Banks, Lisa Delpit, Geneva Gay, Carl A. Grant, Jacqueline Jordan Irvine, Joyce E. King, and William F. Tate. These magnificent scholars gave unselfishly of their time and energy to participate in the interviews, to read and comment on the drafts of their chapters, and to be vulnerable to what I hope will be a wide readership.

I also must acknowledge the hard work of my transcriber, Pat Klitze, at the University of Wisconsin-Madison. I can think of no more labor-intensive and tedious task in qualitative research than listening to and transcribing hours of audiotaped interviews.

This project was done under special circumstances for me. I wrote it while on leave from my work at the University of Wisconsin-Madison. Thus I must thank my institution, particularly the Department of Curriculum and Instruction. I also must thank the Spencer Foundation whose Small Grants Program helped to provide a portion of the funding for the project. Clearly I must acknowledge the Center for Advanced Study in the Behavioral Sciences at Stanford whose residential fellowship program provided me both the space and the intellectual environment to do this work. Of course, all of the errors and omissions in this work are mine alone.

Finally, but most important, I must acknowledge my family at home in Madison, Wisconsin—my husband Charles and daughter Jessica. They were brave, courageous, and unselfish enough to allow me a year away from them to complete this project. This was not simply an issue of missing a few meals or a few family events. It meant missing out on almost everything, and yet they carried out all of the tasks that make a family function. I can never repay their sacrifice.

ONE

Introduction

The hands are required to be in the cotton fields as soon as it is light in the morning, and, with the exception of ten or fifteen minutes, which is given them at noon to swallow their allowance of cold bacon, they are not permitted to be a moment idle until it is too dark to see . . .

Twelve Years as a Slave:
Narrative of Solomon Northrup (Auburn, N.Y.: 1853)

Missy,...I can remember de days when I was one of de house servants. My old marster was a good man, he treated all of his slaves kind, and took care of dem.... Thank God I had good white folks, dey sho' did trus' me to[o], I had charge of all de keys in the house and I waited on de Missy and de chillun.

Charity Anderson, Mobile, Alabama,
Interviewed by Ila Prine, April 16, 1937

The two quotations at the beginning of this chapter serve as markers for two different experiences of African Americans[1] who endured slavery in the United States. The first quote, from Solomon Northrup, describes the experiences of the masses of enslaved Africans doing labor-intensive plantation and small planter work. This work was grueling, dehumanizing, and nonstop. These enslaved Africans were thought of as "field slaves" (or more pejoratively, "field negras"). The second quote, from Charity Anderson, taken from the Federal Writers' Project, describes the experience of a "house slave"—a step up from the field slave, but a slave just the same. Working in the Big House might provide more creature comforts, but one remained a servant just the same. These positions find analogies for African Americans in the 21st century.

The masses of people are employed in work that provides little personal satisfaction and limited opportunity to influence the social, political, and cultural conditions of the community or world around them. This is not to suggest that such work is not necessary or important. It just fails to inspire and uplift those who do it. We know this work as unskilled or semiskilled labor, clerical work, and low-level management. Similarly, a much smaller and more elite group of people occupy a higher paid, more prestigious kind of work—professionals, managers, entrepreneurs—that may allow greater influence (or provide the illusion of such), personal power, and social impact.

In the case of African Americans, the distinction between field-workers and Big House workers represents an important set of tensions. What responsibilities do those who have access to the "Big House" (or academy, boardroom, or corporate offices) have to those who are left in the fields? What, if anything, can field-workers expect from Big House workers? How do Big House workers make an impact on the Big House such that the Big House is not a goal in and of itself? How can the Big House, so long a symbol of what is wrong in the society, be transformed to better serve those whom society has long ignored?

In a controversial interview on San Diego radio station KFMB-AM, activist and entertainer Harry Belafonte stated, "In the days of slavery, there were those slaves who lived on the plantation and there were those slaves that lived in the house. You got the privilege of living in the house if you served the master . . . exactly the way the master intended to have you serve him" (CNN.com, 2002) Belafonte's reference was to the way Secretary of State Colin Powell was functioning in the George W. Bush Administration.

The media and various officials pilloried Belafonte for his statements, but many African Americans understood the context of his comments. The challenge to succeed in the society while maintaining a close commitment to the uplift of the culture is daunting. Poet Audre Lorde (1981) asserted that "the master's tools will never dismantle the master's house" to underscore the difficulty of using the very institutions that oppress to liberate. However, scholar Henry Louis Gates (1997) argues that the *only* way to dismantle the master's house is with the master's tool. Many African American academics and other scholars of color grapple with the contradiction of being "in the Big House" while not being "of the Big House."

In the next section, I extend the Big House metaphor and begin to describe the particular concerns of teacher education that challenge African American teacher educators.

TEACHER EDUCATION AS THE BIG HOUSE

Historically, teaching has been a stable, high-status profession for the African American middle class (Giddings, 1984). Although African Americans were historically locked out of many middle-class professions such as medicine, law, corporate commerce, and the professorate, teaching and preaching were available to them. Of course, historically they taught and preached to Black people. The teaching and preaching traditions run deep in the African American community. Even in the midst of enslavement, African Americans found ways to feed the mind and the spirit.

Milla Granson, a slave in Kentucky, was taught to read by the children of her owner, even though it was illegal to educate slaves. She then organized a clandestine school, eventually educating hundreds of enslaved African Americans. She carried on this secret project first in Kentucky and then in Louisiana for 7 years, helping many slaves to write freedom passes that allowed them to escape North (Lerner, 1972).

African Americans also preached during enslavement. Both Nat Turner and Richard Allen believed in the spiritual as a vehicle for human liberation (Murphy, 2000). Whereas Turner's spiritual insights led him toward insurrection, Allen founded, along with Absalom Jones, the Free African Society of Philadelphia in 1787, which later became the African Methodist Episcopal Church (Sawyer, 2000).

Although African Americans responded to the twin calls of teaching and preaching, the focus of this volume is solely on the role of African Americans in teaching (in the academy), specifically teacher education. Foster (1997) notes that between 1890 and 1910 the number of Blacks who were employed as teachers rose from 15,100 to 66,236. Further, in the census years of 1890, 1900, and 1910, Black teachers represented more than 40% of Blacks in professional occupations. However, with the exception of those employed at the approximately 100 Historically Black Colleges and Universities (HBCU), few Blacks were (are) employed as teacher educators. Eighty-eight percent of the full-time education professors in the United States are White (American Association of Colleges for Teacher Education, 1994). Eighty-one percent of this faculty is between the ages of 45 and 60 (or older). Except for these statistics, little is written on the lives and experiences of teacher educators. Ducharme (1993) offered an analysis of the teacher education professorate. His study looked at a sample of 34 faculty members—22 males and 12 females at 11 institutions. However, his volume says nothing about any special circumstances that may be attendant to being an African American teacher educator.

In an earlier volume Ducharme and Agne (1989) point out that although teaching is primarily a female profession, most teacher educators are male. Ducharme and Agne argue that the "White male dominance of the faculty of colleges of education remains a relatively undiscussed phenomenon despite the many works dealing with sexism in the academy and the total society" (p. 76).

Zimpher and Sherrill (1996) analyzed 8 years of data from the Research About Teacher Education Project (RATE I–VIII). During that 8-year period the percentage of White faculty remained fairly constant—between 91% and 93%. Of the 8% faculty of color in the RATE database, approximately 5% are African Americans. According to Zimpher and Sherrill (1996), women dominate doctoral programs in education (57%), although they do not dominate the assistant professor rank. Unfortunately, the percentage of students of color in doctoral programs in education remains at less than 10% in traditional doctoral-granting and research I institutions. Thus, as Ducharme and Kluender (1990) observe, "the overwhelming 'maleness' of the faculty is likely to decrease, but the 'whiteness' factor will continue to grow. . . . Those concerned about the lack of correlation between the make-up of teacher education faculty and the nation's ethnic and racial makeup will find no comfort in this study" (p. 46).

Grundy and Hatton (1998) argue that teacher educators' biographies impact their work with teachers, both preservice and in-service. But what do we know about the biographies of most teacher educators? What is it that teacher educators bring to the teacher education experience? Almost 30 years ago, Fuller and Brown (1975) observed:

> Teacher educators, have, by and large, humble social-class origins and low status in comparison with their academic colleagues. They more often hold paying jobs while working toward a degree, enter the faculty later, perhaps with the Ed.D., and so are less likely to have acquired the scholarly credentials valued by academicians. (p. 29).

Ducharme and Agne (1989) conclude that the humble social class origins of education professors may suggest that they are more prone toward parochialism than other academic colleagues. Despite the evidence that suggests that professors of education enjoy less prestige and financial remuneration that of professors in other fields, the fact that they are a part of the academy means that they work in a metaphorical Big House. They share the benefits that accrue to the academy and enjoy the broader community success that comes with being a college or university professor.

Working Conditions in the Big House

Although house slaves were spared the backbreaking fieldwork of picking cotton or other crops in sometimes harsh and oppressive weather conditions, theirs was not necessarily an easy life. Being *in* the house did not mean that one was *of* the house. House slaves were in the house at the pleasure of the master. They were there to work on behalf of the owners, not to enjoy the fruits of such labor. Unfortunately, many African American teacher educators feel a similar tension. They are *in* the academy but not *of* the academy. Their roles are circumscribed by race and the social conditions of African Americans in the broader society.

If one perceives oneself to be working in the Big House, one understands that she or he is there to serve, not to be served. This service may take the form of representing all people of one's racial category. Thus the lone African American teacher educator in a school, college, or department of education becomes the proxy for all African Americans. This person comes to represent the institution's "commitment to diversity." This service also extends to taking responsibility for educating White preservice students about issues of race, class, gender, social justice, and equity. Sleeter (2001) addresses what she terms the "overwhelming presence of whiteness" in teacher education where students of color in these programs begin to feel silenced by the sheer numerical power of White students. Similarly, African American teacher educators are in the midst of the overwhelming presence of whiteness. Their colleagues, their students, the college or university administration, and often the local community are likely to be mostly White.

Permission to stay in the Big House can be tenuous at best. Untenured faculty of color are admonished not to pursue a line of inquiry that interrogates race and other issues of diversity (Frierson, 1990, Padilla, 1994). At the same time, African American teacher educators are expected to teach courses that meet state certification requirements for diversity or multiculturalism and serve as "experts" on such topics. African American teacher educators typically serve as advisers for African American and other students of color. According to Padilla (1994), scholars of color must work under the burden of a "cultural tax" because university administration "assumes that we are best suited for specific tasks because of our race/ethnicity or our presumed knowledge of cultural differences" (p. 26). In addition, Frierson (1990) argues that Black faculty confront the presence of racism within the institution in the form of isolation, lack of mentoring, limited or no access to academic networks, and marginalization of their scholarly ideas. Further, suggests Frierson (1990), the number of African American educational research and teacher education faculty is so small at these schools that the faculty of color are most likely to be judged (for tenure, promotion, and merit) solely by White colleagues.

Derrick Bell's (1987) discussion of academic life as a law professor is illustrative of the experiences of African American professors throughout the academy:

> I liked teaching and writing but I was exhausted and considering resigning. I had become the personal counselor and confidante of virtually all of the Black students and a goodly number of the Whites. The Black students clearly needed someone with whom to share their many problems, and White students, finding

a faculty member actually willing to take time with them, were not reluctant to help keep my appointment book full. I liked the students, but it was hard to give them as much time as they needed. I also had to prepare for classes—where I was expected to give an award-winning performance each day—and serve on every committee at the law school and the university where minority representation was desired. In addition, every emergency involving a racial issue was deemed my problem. I admit I wanted to be involved in these problems, but they all required time and energy. Only another Black law teacher would believe what I had to do to make time for research and writing. (p. 140)

THE PREVAILING THEMES OF AFRICAN AMERICAN TEACHER EDUCATORS' WORK LIVES

This project is steeped in what Lawrence-Lightfoot and Davis (1997) term *portraiture* and as such is less concerned with similarity and congruence than it is with distinctiveness and uniqueness. I seek to tell stories about individuals and their experiences. I try to help the reader better know some well-known and highly respected African American teacher educators. I discuss the methodology of the book in detail in the next chapter. Although my focus is on the uniqueness of the individual teacher educators, it is impossible to ignore the recurring experiences that prompt me to identify several themes.

The Diversity Expert . . . Except When It Matters

The participants in this study represent two cohorts or "generations" of African American teacher educators. One cohort began its work in teacher education during the 1970s, the other began in the 1980s or later. They have done their doctoral level work at some of the nation's best educational research institutions, among them Stanford, Harvard, University of Wisconsin, University of Washington, and University of Texas.

All of the African American teacher educators in the 1970s cohort indicated that they were the first and only African American teacher educators in the schools, colleges, and departments in which they were first employed. This "token" status placed them in the uncomfortable position both of being the institution's proxy for its affirmative action efforts and of being regarded as "diversity experts." Thus in addition to requiring them to fulfill regular teaching, research, and service responsibilities, their institutions called upon them to educate other faculty and community members about issues of race, culture, and ethnicity. The female African American teacher educators were considered "two-fers," in that they satisfied the institution's need to hire more people of color and to hire more women. How these scholars were "counted" in their institutions depended upon how the colleges and universities wanted to represent themselves.

Most of the scholars have conducted "diversity workshops" for their departments, schools, colleges, or universities.[2] The scholars in this study were charged with educating their colleagues and administrators about dealing with the racial, ethnic, cultural, and linguistic changes that were occurring on their campuses. Also, these African American teacher educators often were called upon to be the "public face" of their institutions to local K–12 schools and other community entities. However, these same scholars have been criticized for doing research that was "too ethnic" or, more specifically, "too Black." Thus in the arena where expertise is most valued in the academy—research and scholarship—African American teacher educators have been discouraged from pursuing their interests. This academic pigeonholing happens often to African Americans (and other scholars of color) despite their academic disciplines. Henry Louis Gates and Cornel West are almost always called upon to be the public voice on issues of race and all things African American in the United States. However, Gates is an English professor and West is a philosopher and theologian. When have we heard from Gates on Western literature despite the fact that this is one of his areas of expertise? When do the media ask West to comment on the philosophic or religious values of the nation? Similarly, scholars such as Shelby Steele and John McWhorter have stepped outside of their respective areas of expertise, English and linguistics, respectively, to become apologists for the political right in their attacks on social policies such as affirmative action and other diversity efforts. Their limited knowledge of the social sciences is not considered; their assignment to the Black racial category is enough to give them authority to be racial spokesmen.

You're Not Like the Others . . . You Just Speak for Them

The reason some enslaved Africans were chosen to be house slaves is tied to a notion of exceptionality. Plantation owners determined that some characteristic (or set of characteristics) made one qualified to be a house slave. These characteristics may have been physical (with mixed-raced Africans being more prized), social, or idiosyncratic. Thus the offspring of a rape or illicit sexual liaison might be made a house slave. The mother of a master's slave children may have enjoyed special social status, or an enslaved African who was privy to family secrets might "enjoy the privilege" of working as a house slave. According to historian John Hope Franklin (1988), the house servant group tended to perpetuate itself because the prospect of working in the field was "frowned upon and resisted with every resource at [one's] disposal" (p. 117).

Thus African Americans in the academy recognize that they exist in a kind of "in-between" world between the power and privilege of the social order and the oppression and degradation of their racial group. Residing in the academy is both a privilege and a burden. Clearly it is a privilege because of the attendant perquisites, but it is also a burden because it invites a closer, less forgiving examination of one's competence.

Indeed teaching in the academy is deemed a prize job and the selection of African American (and other scholars of color) teacher educators tends to require a higher level of scrutiny than that applied to their White colleagues (De la luz Reyes & Halcón, 1988). For example, in the hiring process I am struck by the contrast in the participation of my colleagues in interviews and job talks given by scholars of color versus those given by White candidates. My job talk attracted so large an audience that it had to be moved to a larger room. Of course, one might argue that the increased participation represented enthusiasm and interest. But considering that possibility in concert with a number of other factors, I have come to read it as increased scrutiny. When White candidates come, we sometimes have difficulty convening enough colleagues to attend their presentations and interviews. None of the candidates of color who have visited my department during my 12 years there have had to face small audiences nor have they experienced gaps in their interview schedules.

One of the participants in this project referred to an instance at his university where two candidates were being interviewed for the same position. The first candidate was a White male. The participant described this young man's interview as a "love fest," whereas the African American candidate had a much less cordial experience:

> They just couldn't get enough of him [the White candidate]. Their conversations with him sounded like he was already hired. "What would you like to teach? How can we further your research? What things would be most important in encouraging you to select this university?" However, when the African American candidate came they went into an interrogation mode. Their questions rose to a whole other level. "Tell us about the theoretical foundation of your work? How is that kind of work going to fit in with what we do here? Do you think your work is fundable?" Finally, I had enough and just said, "Whoa, why does the Black candidate have to have a 'theoretical framework' and the White candidate is asked about what he'd like to teach?" People could see I was steaming over this and of course they came sneaking back around to me to tell me how "sorry" they were if I thought the candidate was being treated differently since that was not their intent. I couldn't go on intent. I went on what I saw happening and what was happening wasn't fair. (field notes, April 12, 2002)

The selection of African American teacher educators often amounts to searching for academic stars. Much like Karen's (1990) findings about who gets into elite colleges and universities like Harvard, African American teacher educators who get into the academy (particularly into the elite academy) are also seen as a "special" class. The special-ness is not merely about one's intellectual acumen or educational pedigree. Rather, it is about a sense of how good a "fit" the African American teacher educator will have with the current community of scholars. Thus African American teacher educators find themselves perceived as "different from the rest" but able to provide a window on the thoughts and feelings of the rest of their racial category.

Several of the African American teacher educators in this book commented that during the national spectacle of the O. J. Simpson murder trial, they were asked by colleagues and members of their institutional community, "Well, what do Black people think about this trial" (or verdict, or O. J. Simpson himself)? Besides being insulting from the standpoint of homogenizing all African Americans into one monolithic mindset, such comments also reflect the failure of White faculty members to enter into genuine relationships with African American colleagues. The Simpson question (and others like it) serves as an ongoing barometer of whether or not the scholar of color continues to fit into the institution.

Participants in this project also spoke about the sense of being "on display" for their schools, colleges, and departments. In addition to being the institutions' proxies for affirmative action (as mentioned above), African American teacher educators felt that they were being presented to say, "See, she or he is just like us," because of his or her ability to "fit in" the institutional environment. The work of fitting in can be stressful and challenging. On campuses where there are few scholars of color, African American teacher educators may experience an uncomfortable need to demonstrate solidarity with all other scholars of color, even when they may disagree. On one major university campus the university president learned that a "star" African American scholar was being wooed away by another university. "Well, what do you want?" asked the president. "What can convince you to stay?" The African American scholar calmly and carefully replied, "I want there to be enough Black scholars on this campus that I don't have to like them all!" The scholar succinctly described the perennial dilemma of African American teacher educators. If one is the only Black scholar in the department and an additional African American scholar is hired, the two often feel compelled to present a united front on a variety of issues so that neither is used against the other in subsequent circumstances. One of the participants was the only African American scholar on a national panel. When she raised some substantive questions about the direction of the work, she was confronted by a comment that "Professor 'So and So' (another African American scholar) agrees with us." She noted, "It's as if there is only one Black mind out there and if you disagree with that, you lose your Black card. What's interesting is that such cards are being bestowed and rescinded by White people!"

In another instance, a senior scholar told of his attempt to assist a young, untenured African American colleague:

> I tried to help her because I could see she was headed for trouble [concerning her tenure]. She didn't want to be seen as a "Black" scholar and she did whatever she could to avoid me. I wasn't trying to date her or trying to get her to join an alliance with me to overthrow the department. I was just trying to be a colleague. Her failure to use me as a resource—I've been here a long time—caused her to make some poor decisions. In the end, the White friendships she was trying to cultivate didn't help her get tenure. She tearfully came to me years later when she was denied tenure to say, "I should have listened to you." (personal conversation, November 20, 1999)

The Work Is Too Narrow...But, Really It's Too Black

At an invited academic conference a Latina researcher raised a question about what the researchers were trying to do with their teaching and learning innovations. "Are you trying to get the children to be like you, or are you trying to get them to be the best 'them' they can be?" Several of the White researchers seemed puzzled by her questions, while a look of recognition came over the faces of the scholars of color present, for they too experience a similar choice. The work of the academy often requires scholars to conform to established canons in order to become the progeny of mainstream scholars who have come before. However, contemporary African American teacher educators are attempting to ask new research questions and create new research paradigms. This kind of work is not without risk. Top-tier journals tend to be more conservative and prefer to publish work that fits more comfortably in the familiar research genres. African American teacher educators face the challenge of trying to break new epistemological and methodological ground and getting their work reviewed and published in the more prestigious journals.

One of the participants in this project explained that when she was preparing for her tenure review, she spent a lot of time and energy educating her department's promotion and tenure review committee about the nature of her work and the publication outlets she had chosen for her work:

> I don't know what other people do when they put their tenure files

together but I had to get the committee to see that my work was bigger than tenure and promotion. I was going to do this work whether I was a professor or not because it's bigger than an academic exercise. It's about the survival of a people. (field notes, May 22, 1999)

This more politicized nature of the work of African American teacher educators places them in jeopardy of not receiving tenure and/or promotion. The demand for so-called objective or neutral scholarship makes almost no sense to many African American teacher educators who are keenly aware of the pitiful educational conditions many African American students endure. Their work may point directly toward "the survival of a people" and, as such, must reflect a position of advocacy and political urgency.

Also, the possibility of blatant racism still exists in the academy. Professor Reginald Clark's celebrated case (see Shea, 1992) illustrates the lengths to which a faculty will go to deny others entrance into the academy. While working late one night in his office, Clark overheard his colleagues discussing his case. The committee's voices carried through the building's ductwork, and what he heard shocked him. Clark had the presence of mind to tape-record the conversation wherein his colleagues expressed concern about granting tenure to a Black man. As a result of a lawsuit, Clark was awarded $1.4 million in damages against the university.

Clark's case is important because the public discussion was that his work was inadequate. However, there was little discussion of his book on African American family life and school achievement (1984) that served as a challenge to deficit paradigm work on African American students and their families. Mr. Clark was seeking tenure at an institution that had at that time no African American faculty members with tenure, and he brought with him a research agenda specifically focused on African Americans. The fact that he was successful in meeting the established standards of scholarship did not protect Clark from the racism that existed among his colleagues in his department.

All of the participants in this study have a research agenda that addresses culture, social justice, and education. Most of them focus their work specifically on the education (and liberation) of African Americans. Most have been challenged at some time in their careers about this focus. One participant pointed out that although she has interests in "multicultural education," her primary focus is on the education of African American students. "More than one colleague, dean, or department chair has commented that I should include more 'multicultural' work because my work will be seen as too narrow. I understand that to mean my work is 'too black'!"

CONCLUSION

In this first chapter I have relied on the metaphor of the Big House to describe the academic lives of African American teacher educators. By making comparisons to the living conditions of enslaved Africans, I have attempted to make sense of the paradoxical relationship that African American scholars (and other scholars of color) have with the academy. Far from having "made it," African American teacher educators are aware of the terms and conditions under which they are permitted in the academy. Others such as Lubrano (2003), Dews and Law (1995), and Tokarczyk and Fay (1993) have written in a compelling fashion about the ambivalence that working-class scholars have about their class privilege in the academy and their class identity in family and social relationships. However, not one of these volumes focuses exclusively on African American scholars, and none focuses exclusively on teacher educators.

The scholars who participated in the interviews also face the challenges of legitimacy and authenticity in the larger African American community, particularly those segments of the community that remain on the economic, political, and educational margins. All of these scholars do work designed to better serve the causes of social justice, equity, and eradicating racism. Some are more deliberately focused on African Americans in the course of their work, whereas others take a more multicultural, multi-ethnic approach.

In the subsequent chapters, I discuss the methodology of this project, the individual participants and their work, and the conclusions I have drawn from this project.

NOTES

1. I will be using the terms *African American* and *Black* interchangeably throughout this book.

2. Some of the scholars in large state institutions have done this work for entire state university systems.

TWO

The Method and the Madness

What I Did and Why I Did It

> *"I've always believed that a portrait captures a person better than a photograph. It takes a real human being to see another human being."*
>
> Sean P. Diddy Combs in "Monster's Ball"
> (Paseornek & Forster, 2001)

As I stated in the previous chapter, Sara Lawrence-Lightfoot is well known for the use of what researchers term *portraiture* (Lawrence-Lightfoot & Davis, 1997). It is a methodological technique that challenges the researcher to "paint" rich renderings of a subject. According to Lawrence-Lightfoot, "portraiture is a method of qualitative research that blurs the boundaries of aesthetics and empiricism in an effort to capture the complexity, dynamics, and subtlety of human experience and organizational life" (p. xv). Featherstone (1989) suggests that portraiture links the voices and perspectives of narrators, storytellers, and the audience. It is a form of scholarship that includes both "analytic rigor" and "community building." Indeed, according to Featherstone, portraiture is "a people's scholarship" where "scientific facts gathered in the field give voice to a people's experience" (p. 375).

But scholars using portraiture are not interested merely in painting rich pictures or telling good stories. They are compelled by more than the desire to represent complex descriptions of the context, the setting, and the people. Rather, portraitists also work to unearth a central story and an "authentic narrative" (Lawrence-Lightfoot & Davis, 1997, p. 12). This technique is both complicated and complex. It is complicated because it involves many layers of investigation and analysis. It is complex because it contains no predictable pattern of work. What appears to be a simple and straightforward question has the potential to lead to wondrous explorations and unforeseen outcomes.

Because of its complexity, a full examination of portraiture is not possible in this chapter. Rather, this chapter focuses on aspects of the researcher's role in developing portraits. Lawrence-Lightfoot (Lawrence-Lightfoot & Davis, 1997) suggests that the researcher is made more visible and evident in portraiture: "She is seen not only in defining the focus and field of the inquiry, but also in navigating the relationships with the subjects, in witnessing and interpreting the action, in tracing the emergent themes, and in creating the narrative" (p. 13).

Creating a narrative and navigating the relationship with the participants are part of the foci of this book. I attempt to look at how African American teacher educators negotiate and make sense of their work in the academy. I attempt to look at the contradictions of an enterprise that professes a commitment to equity and diversity while simultaneously excluding these elements in its own practices and enactments. I think these practices are a part of the discursive moves that characterize teacher education. I think of the discursive moves of teacher education as important tools for portraying what teacher education is to potential teachers, practicing teachers, other teacher educators, and the education community writ large.

The following discussion about teacher education discourse is important in my work with African American teacher educators because the reader must keep in mind the context of teacher education in which these teacher educators work. Although this discourse impacts everyone involved in teacher education, it creates a particular tension for African American teacher educators who have dedicated their scholarly careers to equity, social justice, and fighting racism and other forms of oppression. The particular tension is tied to the African American teacher educators' embodiment of race and what they come to represent in the academy. Thus if they fail to take up this discourse, they may be seen as out of step with the standards and conventions of the profession. If they fail to challenge this discourse, they may be seen as so fully assimilated into the system—so much a part of the Big House—that they are incapable of affecting change.

To develop my argument about the discursive moves of teacher education I call upon more popular culture symbols such as film. There is a moment in the film *The Wizard of Oz* where Dorothy and her traveling companions are in search of the Wicked Witch's broom. Frightened out of his wits during their harrowing journey, the Cowardly Lion declares, "I do believe in ghosts—I do, I do, I do." The lion's chant may be compared to teacher education's discursive declarations. First, I must be clear that I do believe that teacher education matters. Like Darling-Hammond (with her work with the National Commission on Teaching and America's Future, 1996), I concur that teacher education makes a difference in the quality of education students are likely to experience. However, NCTAF also calls for the reinvention of teacher education.

My argument is directed at the majority of teacher education and the cant it deploys in the preparation of teachers. I use a definition of *cant* that refers to "a set or stock phrase; the expression or repetition of conventional, trite or unconsidered opinions or sentiments; especially the insincere use of pious phraseology" (see *Webster's New World Collegiate Dictionary*, 1977). The teacher education cant is subtle. It is not merely repetition of phrases and dogma. Rather, it is the re-inscription of certain behaviors, attitudes, and performances by teacher educators that are rewarded or sanctioned that help novice teachers understand what should be valued. The African American teacher educators in this project regularly found themselves working against these cants with little or no support from their colleagues, their institutions, and/or the profession.

The following are examples of the teacher education cant:

- Good teachers are created as a result of (preservice) teacher education.
- There is a "right" way to teach.
- Teachers are preparing students for the "real" world.
- Good teaching can operate separate from student learning.
- Student failure typically results from student, parent, community or cultural shortcomings, and/or dysfunction.
- It is enough for some students to have a "good experience" in the classroom.

What follows is a brief explication of how each cant listed above is deployed in teacher education and its relationship to the work of African American teacher educators:

Good teachers are created as a result of (preservice) teacher education. This first cant forms the entire basis for teacher education. Although I asserted above that teacher education matters, I do not mean to confuse preparation with perfection. Teacher education relies on a rhetoric of perfecting a product. Prospective teachers come to believe that by being admitted into a program, taking the requisite courses, and successfully completing the fieldwork, they become good teachers. Rather than emphasizing the reality of their novice status, teacher education often positions new teachers as the innovators and change agents that teaching needs. The message that teacher education students hear is that it is their job to pull the profession out of its antiquated, stagnant practice. They are thought to be able to do this because of their teacher education. Rarely are teacher education students introduced to the idea that in order to become good teachers, they will need both experience and ongoing education. An indicator of the prevalence of this discourse is the way that program rankings presume teaching excellence. Teachers who went to Program X are thought to be better than those who went to Program Y. These presumptions almost never look carefully at the student profiles of particular programs that might suggest that some programs recruit and serve a higher proportion of high achievers (as measured by grades and standardized test scores).

Haberman (1995) argues that teachers prepared to teach in urban schools serving large numbers of children in poverty (and children of color) need to come to teacher education with something—experience, empathy, and/or expertise. Thus he has argued against trying to create teachers through teacher education. Haberman's (1995) work represents an almost wholesale rejection of traditional teacher education. Most mainstream teacher educators reject his notion that undergraduates cannot and should not be recruited for multicultural, urban teaching. Below I give a brief description of these cants and how they operate in teacher education.

African American teacher educators may be presumed to be less capable of preparing students for the classrooms in which they ultimately want to teach, that is, schools serving White, middle-class students. If students internalize this cant that teacher education is where "I become a good teacher," they may express doubts and concerns about whether African American teacher educators are the right people to prepare them, particularly those students who have never had a teacher of color. In an earlier article (Ladson-Billings, 1996) I reported on my experiences as a Black teacher in a class of all White students. Despite my decade of public school teaching experience, students often treated me in ways that challenged my legitimacy. How were they going to learn to be "good" teachers if they were not learning from a "good" teacher?

There is a "right" way to teach. This cant is evident in what kinds of performances are rewarded during teacher education. If prospective students use specified rubrics and methods, they are rewarded. If they do not, they are sanctioned. As Delpit (1995) argues, many of the progressive techniques she learned in her teacher education program failed to help improve the education of the African American children in her classroom. However, her White colleagues encouraged her to continue to use teaching methods that seemed alien to the children who needed her most.

Another example of this notion of a "right" way to teach is that of the early iterations of the National Board for Professional Teaching Standards (NBPTS) assessments. NBPTS clearly rewarded teachers who used a middle-class, "progressive" teaching approach over those who used a more direct, "traditional" approach (Ladson-Billings, 2000). My argument is not to create stark dichotomies between teaching styles, because such binaries invariably leave us in warring ideological camps that totally ignore students' needs. Rather, I want to suggest that when we privilege one form of teaching, we simplify and trivialize what is a complex and deeply significant undertaking. Teaching and learning involve constant negotiation and re-creation. Not only is there not just one way to teach, but many teachers vary in how they teach different concepts, ideas, and subjects, or how they teach different learners.

African American teacher educators may bring a different teaching repertoire to the classroom. They may be more direct in their questioning, more exacting in their requirements, or more expressive in their presentation. This is not to suggest that there is a stereotypical Black teacher who exhibits a "Black teaching style." Rather, I argue that some of the collective experiences of Black life may find their way into the classroom, just as the home, community, and cultural experiences of White teachers influence their classrooms. For example, Foster's (1989) description of an African American community college teacher details the teacher's use of African American colloquialisms and sermonic style to motivate and relate to her students.

If students presume there is but one way to teach, they may grow impatient and intolerant of any teacher (and his or her teaching) who deviates from the assumed norm.

Teachers are preparing students for the "real" world. Another persistent discourse in teacher education is that school is a place where teachers prepare students for the "real" world. One can only assume that this thinking posits school and students' lives as existing in some "unreal" world for students. For many students school is the unreal world. Its language, rules, and practices do not resemble anything that people engaged in day-to-day living participate in. Sometimes that world is harsh and unyielding, and sometimes that world is protected and filled with resources, but make no mistake, it is the real world of the students' experiences.

I suspect that this discourse of preparation for the real world is tied to the notion that schools as institutions have a difficult time justifying what they do. When students respond with their oft-heard cry, "Why do we have to learn this stuff?" teachers generally say something like, "You're going to need this someday (or next year, or when you get a job, or in high school)." Rarely are the skills, knowledge, and attitudes being promulgated in schools thought to be of use in the everyday, current lives of students. Schools treat students as if their lives are insignificant and incidental to learning—as if their lives are unreal and on hold. School sets itself up as a vehicle to the real world, and students often see it as an inconvenient detour.

African American teacher educators' biographies and backgrounds may create for them a dual existence within and beyond the academy. They know that although the two spaces are different worlds, they are both very real. The idea that the work of teaching is preparing students for the "real" world stands in opposition to a notion of multiple worlds that are complex, nested, overlapping, and messy. The African American teacher educators who participated in this project negotiate a variety of worlds, and each has its own set of challenges. Most began these negotiations early in their lives when they were children. They understand that school may help prepare students for future schooling and life in the workplace. However, they also understand that students are already grappling with the real world.

Good teaching can occur separate from student learning. Because teacher education typically rewards the "performances" of preservice teachers, little emphasis is placed on student learning. The supervision of student teaching involves having a university-based supervisor come to the classroom to watch and evaluate the performance. I can think of no instances where student teachers are held accountable for student learning as a condition of certification. This practice of rewarding performances is carried over into in-service teaching where administrators continue to reward those teachers who demonstrate the "right" kind of teaching. Unfortunately, it has taken draconian accountability measures to link student achievement with teacher performance. These measures reduce student achievement to standard scores that shrink the full range of school learning.

Similarly, in the early National Board certification process, a large portion of the assessment relied on teacher performance.[1] There are limited instances where teachers are asked to show student work but almost no instances where the achievement of the students is tied to the granting of National Board certification. Indeed, the most privileged skill in NBPTS certification is writing. Those teachers who write well (regardless of their students' academic achievement) are more likely to become certified. Clearly, any teacher who has the patience and stamina to undergo the yearlong certification process is likely to be someone who thinks deeply and carefully about teaching. Such a person may be a good teacher, but not necessarily. Unfortunately, we continue to uncouple students' learning from teaching.

The African American teacher educators in this project regularly raised questions about student learning. As one participant remarked (about the proliferation of scholarly publications and research activities), "If there are these many smart folks (in education), why are the kids so dumb?" One of the persistent questions among African American teacher educators is, How is it that so much experimentation and supposed innovation take place in schools serving poor, urban students of color, and yet so little learning results?

Student failure typically results from student, parent, community, or cultural shortcomings and/or dysfunction. This particular cant pervades teacher education. The courses, the texts, and the experiences all are aimed at addressing some alleged pathology on the part of the students, their families, their communities, and/or their cultures. The school quickly imperializes the space of normalcy, and any students who do not conform to that space are thought to have abnormalities that emanate from outside of the school in the "dangerous, chaotic worlds" of their families and communities.

The teacher education discourse of diversity often serves as the major promoter of this cant. From the time they enter teacher education programs, prospective teachers begin to hear about the "problem" (or "challenge") of teaching diverse students. They hear about poverty, family dissolution, strange cultural practices, and any number of things to instantiate their own normative positions. Often prospective teachers are asked to select a student to "study," and many times such focal students are selected for the degrees of difference they represent from the mainstream.

Many preservice teachers see field experiences in diverse classrooms as something they must endure in order to complete a program, and such assignments may magnify the fears and anxieties students already have about teaching the "other." In the teacher education program in which I work, a young White woman placed in a middle school serving diverse students had an African American sixth-grade boy in her class she regularly ignored and allowed to fail. On a day when the supervisor was observing the preservice teacher, the supervisor noted that the little boy was not doing any work. After about 15 minutes into the activity, the boy made his way to the teacher's desk and asked for a pencil. The preservice teacher told the boy that she was not going to give him a pencil and that he should try to borrow one from a classmate. The boy proceeded to ask other students, one at a time, whether or not they had a pencil he could use. After about 16 of his classmates refused him, someone finally gave him a pencil.

By the time the boy sat down with his newly proffered pencil, the class hour was over. During the postobservation conference the supervisor asked, "What was going on between you and D'Andre?" The student teacher answered, "Oh, I don't really do much with him. I'm afraid of him!" The supervisor exclaimed, "He's 10!"

This fear of the other, although perhaps not as explicitly acknowledged by other prospective teachers, permeates and is cultivated by teacher education. It is coupled with constant reminders of the limited abilities and need to dilute the curriculum and compromise learning for children defined as the

Other. Parents of the Other are unable to garner support for their children. If these parents do not come to school, they are cast as neglectful and not valuing education. If they do come to school, they are seen as threatening and intimidating. No matter what they do, they are seen as the reason for their children's school failure.

African American teacher educators have been challenging this particular cant for many years. It arises out of the deficit paradigm that produced public policy and compensatory education programs to remind us that poor children and children of color were somehow not quite as good as White, middle-class children. Although African American teacher educators may represent exceptions in the college or university classroom, they also represent a kind of proof. The fact that they are in the academy means that it is possible for African American students to succeed in school. Their mere presence should erode beliefs about the presumed deficiencies inherent in race, class, and culture.

It is enough for some students to have a "good experience" in the classroom. Teacher education cant often focuses on the "quality of experience"—were the students made to feel welcome, were they included, did they have fun, was the teacher nice to them—while simultaneously paying little or no attention to the quality of education students receive. The quality of experience rhetoric urges prospective teachers to create warm, friendly classrooms (which, of course, no one can argue against), but such urging can mask the import of student learning and its primacy in the classroom.

In classrooms focused on student learning for diverse students (Ladson-Billings, 1994), teachers point out the urgency of attending to student learning. Being a "warm fuzzy" teacher is a secondary concern. However, teacher education repeatedly focuses on preparing teachers who are "nice" to students regardless of how little students may be learning in their classrooms. It is interesting to me that in classrooms serving high-status, mainstream students, teachers find a way to be both "nice" and demanding, and when forced to choose, many parents choose demanding.

African American teacher educators often take up the challenge of helping prospective students understand that poor children of color are both different from and the same as their White counterparts. They are different because of the historical and social contexts of racism, discrimination, and oppression that place them in a different relationship to schools as institutions. Yet they are the same in that their parents, families, and communities have similar aspirations for academic and career success. The participants in this study regularly returned to a theme of making sure poor children of color measured up and displayed academic excellence.

HOW THE INTERVIEWS DEVELOPED

In an earlier paper (Ladson-Billings, 2003) I compared teacher education and its attempts to deal with the preparation of teachers for schools and classrooms serving our increasingly diverse cities and towns with the movie classic *The Wizard of Oz*. I point out that the profession treats the preservice teachers like "Munchkins" and attempts to send everybody "somewhere, over the rainbow." However, I think of this project with African American teacher educators to be more like the 1978 Quincy Jones production *The Wiz*—a modern day, urban version of *The Wizard of Oz*. This new twist on Oz is a metaphor for the potential that African American teacher educators have in remaking the profession. I have seen their work as a potential rupture of the "business as usual" policies and the rhetorical cants of teacher education tradition. To explore this possibility I began conducting pilot interviews of African American teacher educators to learn more about their experiences, insights, and impact on the field.

Originally, I cast a broad net for African American teacher educators. I used resources and databases from the Research Focus on Black Education Special Interest Group of the American Educational Research Association, Historically Black Colleges and Universities, Black Special Interest Groups from the National Council of Teachers of English, the National Council for the Social Studies, and the National Council for Teachers of Mathematics.

I did two pilot interviews to determine how long the interviews might take and how effective my questions were at getting at the issues that were most important for this book. My initial interview was with a colleague with whom I have no personal or professional relationship. Although the participant did an excellent job of responding to my questions, the formal nature of our interaction made for what I saw as a stilted and somewhat artificial setting. Because my work has historically involved long-term, in situ research, short-term interviewing did not appear to yield exactly what I was after.

My second interview was with a colleague I have known for many years. The quality of that interview was amazing. I was certain I already knew everything there was to know about this colleague and yet this interview revealed so much more. I kept asking additional questions and kept getting new perspectives. This interview helped me better shape the ones that followed. It probably gave me the frame in which to set this work. At the close of that interview I decided that my participants would be only colleagues I knew well and that I would limit their number in the event that I needed to return to interview them over time.

I selected seven African American teacher educators with whom I have ongoing relationships. These are relationships cultivated over many years—

graduate school, professional associations, research and scholarship, political participation, community organizing. I looked for scholar/colleagues who were in a variety of institutional circumstances—research and doctoral-granting institutions, small colleges, predominately White institutions and historically Black institutions, males and females, mid-career professionals and veteran professionals. I looked to those I knew well because many of the stories they told would be familiar, and at the same moment they would be comfortable enough with me to share some of their life's narrative that had never before been revealed. As Featherstone (1989) argues, "The telling of stories can be a profound form of scholarship moving serious study close to the frontiers of art in the capacity to express complex truth and moral context in intelligible ways" (p. 377). And Lawrence-Lightfoot and Davis (1997) point out that "the portrait . . . creates a narrative that is at once complex, provocative, and inviting that attempts to be holistic, revealing the dynamic interaction of values, personality, structure, and history" (p. 11).

Lawrence-Lightfoot (Lawrence-Lightfoot & Davis, 1997) also details the role of the researcher in portraiture research and points out that whereas ethnographers listen *to* a story, portraitists listen *for* a story. Thus the role of the researcher in portraiture is active and engaged. This activity and engagement do not mean that the researcher is permitted to select or identify the story but is expected to "shape the story's coherence and aesthetic" (pp. 12–13).

I am implicated throughout this book. I have chosen not only to study people who do what I do but also to study people who share my racial category. Further, I have chosen to write about intimates. The participants in this project are important to me on both professional and personal levels. My connection to them requires me to maintain the highest ethical standards (Bell, 2002) to preserve both levels of our relationship.

Again citing Lawrence-Lightfoot (Lawrence-Lightfoot & Davis, 1997), "Portraiture admits the central and creative role of the *self* of the portraitist" (p. 13). But the researcher must be true to the data and apply appropriate methodological tools to the creation of the narrative. Even with this adherence to methodological canons, the researcher remains visible:

> With portraiture, the person of the researcher—even when vigorously controlled—is more evident and more visible than in any other research form. She is seen not only in defining the focus and field of the inquiry, but also in navigating the relationships with the subjects, in witnessing and interpreting the action, in tracing the emergent themes, and in creating the narrative. (p. 13)

Creating a narrative and navigating the relationship with the participants was one of the foci of this book. The nature of my relationship with each of the participants in this project is crucial. Several years ago a White colleague commented that she had attended a "special group" meeting of teacher educators and asked why there were no teacher educators of color in attendance. A reply came back, "Well, we don't know any teacher educators of color." The colleague beseeched me to apply for membership to this group. My application would need endorsement from two or three current members of the group. The irony of having to ask people who participate in an exclusionary group to include me is stunning. How can people get in (and gain access) when the gatekeepers dedicate their energy and efforts to keeping them out? More important, that a scholar of repute claimed not to even know any teacher educators of color forced me to not only recollect who the teacher educators of color are but also document their experiences in teacher education for a much wider audience.

This book is a confluence of context, voice, relationship, and the emergent themes identified in Chapter 1. The analytic tool or rubric I used to construct this narrative is what scholar Sylvia Wynter (1992) refers to as "alterity." Alterity refers to the alter ego category of otherness that is specific to each culture's "metaphor of the self." Wynter argues that those constructed as "the other" have a perspective advantage. This advantage does not speak to the economic, social, and political disadvantage that subordinated groups may experience but rather to the way that not being positioned in the center allows for a "wide-angle" vision. According to King (1995), this advantage is not due to an inherent racial/cultural difference but is the result of the dialectical nature of the constructed otherness that prescribes the liminal status of people of color as beyond the normative boundary of Self/Other.

Those who occupy the liminal position do not seek to move from the margins to the mainstream because they understand the corrupting influences of the mainstream—its pull to maintain status quo relations of power and inequities. Rather, the work of the liminal perspective is to reveal the ways that dominant perspectives distort the realities of the other in an effort to maintain power relations that continue to disadvantage those who are locked out of the mainstream.

This book is about sharing the views of teacher educators who are working both within and against institutional constraints of specific workspaces (i.e., colleges and universities) and the profession (i.e., teacher educators). It is about what it means to have a vision that is beyond the Big House.

My own theoretical orientation has been informed by what King and Mitchell (1990/1995) call a "culture-centered" approach that "charges us with the responsibility to know ourselves and educate ourselves from the inside" (p. 7). It also is informed by Patricia Hill Collins's (1991) notion of an "Afrocentric feminist epistemology." I am not interested in positivist notions of "objectivity," presumptions of "normality," or replication. Rather, I am concerned with authenticity or, as young African Americans say, "keepin' it real." To achieve this authenticity I have to stay in close contact with the participants and be willing to have them critique and correct my explication of the narrative.

As I embark on what for me is a new methodology—portraiture--I am once again struck by Lawrence-Lightfoot's (Lawrence-Lightfoot & Davis, 1997) insights on this way of working:

> Portraiture is a method framed by the traditions and values of the phenomenological paradigm, sharing many of the techniques, standards, and goals of ethnography. But it pushes against the constraints of those traditions and practices in its explicit effort to combine empirical and aesthetic description, in its focus on the convergence of narrative and analysis, in its goal of speaking to broader audiences beyond the academy (thus linking inquiry to public discourse and social transformation), in its standard of authenticity rather than reliability and validity (the traditional standards of quantitative and qualitative inquiry), and in its explicit recognition of the use of the self as the primary research instrument for documenting and interpreting the perspectives and experiences of the people and the cultures being studied. (pp. 13–14)

THE TECHNICAL DETAILS

Whereas I have offered a few of the specifics of the interviews previously, in this section I share more of the mundane aspects of "doing the work." Although I am less interested in writing about this aspect of my work, I recognize that such details are important for young scholars who are struggling to craft their own programs of research. I asked each participant where she or he would feel most comfortable having the interview conducted. This may seem to be a simple detail, but the establishment of rapport often grows out of a researcher's care and concerns for the desires of the participant. I interviewed participants in their offices, in a hotel room where one was staying to attend a meeting, in a hotel lobby where another was attending a conference, in a meeting room, and over the telephone. In other words, I was willing to meet the participants when they were available and wherever they were.

I audiotaped each interview and took notes throughout. I listened to the tapes after the interview and took additional notes. I then allowed a professional transcriber to transcribe the tapes and send them to me in electronic files that could be downloaded into the NVivo qualitative software for analysis. I organized the data according to some emergent themes and reorganized the information according to the metaphor of the Big House around which the project was developing. In the end, I decided that the Big House metaphor helped me construct a more coherent narrative about the experiences of African American teacher educators.

In the subsequent chapters, I tell each participant's story and construct that participant in relation to a significant actual or literary personality from African and/or African American history and culture. This is a liberty I have exercised as the portraitist. I believe it helps the reader know the participant better, and it helps create a collective story of struggle and triumph. I must emphasize that these personality comparisons are mine. Just as the outstanding teachers I identified in my earlier book, *The Dreamkeepers* (Ladson-Billings, 1994), would never call themselves "dreamkeepers" or "Culturally Relevant" teachers, these colleagues did not assume these personalities. I have assigned them as a way to carry the narrative. It is my hope that they convey the power, influence, and integrity these scholars exert on the field and on me personally. The characterizations are meant as an homage, and I trust that both they and the readers will take them as such.

One caution I must offer about my rendering of the participants' words is that it is important to remember that words on a page, even when they are verbatim statements, cannot fully capture the speaker's meaning and connotation. To attempt to bring out some of the richness and accuracy of their words, I have edited the transcriptions liberally. Because readers will not have benefit of the live interview or audiotapes, as translator I have used a variety of punctuation and stylistic tools to better convey the participants' words, ideas, and meanings. I assume responsibility for any errors in meaning and regret that readers will not have the wonderful pleasure of hearing the words as they were uttered.

NOTE

1. An African American teacher who successfully completed the NBPTS certification process contacted me to ask me to look at her assessment materials to determine whether or not her students were "learning anything." She indicated that she thought that very little in the assessment addressed student learning, which was her primary concern.

THREE

Joyce King

Yemajá

Many scholars have written about the cultural connections of people of African descent (Asante, 1987; Gay & Baber, 1987; Richards, 1985). One of the more enduring connections is the spiritual one. Although discussions about European and American enslavement of Africa imply that Africans were either without religious tradition or that those traditions were based on superstition and idolatry, the historical and cultural records indicate "religion has always been a vital part of Black life in both Africa and the United States" (Karenga, 2000, p. 41). One of the oldest religious traditions in Africa is that of Yoruba. The influence of space, time, and circumstance forced enslaved Africans to transform their religious traditions into new forms of spirituality. In the Americas one of the transformations was into Regla de Ocha or Santeria, developed mostly in Cuba.

Fundamental to the religion is the idea that through divination, proper character, and appropriate behavior, one can improve one's life on earth rather than in an afterlife. Clearly in the midst of the horror of slavery, this was seen as a relevant religious practice. The religion is based on belief in one god, the creator, along with a number of deities or Orishas that represent a variety of forces of nature—lightning, wind, water—or principles. Some of the Orishas have historical connections, tying them to actual historical figures that displayed special character and accomplishments.

The Orishas have been compared to the saints of Catholicism, and during slavery in the Caribbean, enslaved Africans disguised their worship of Orishas as prayers to saints. One of the Orishas is a female named Yemajá. She is considered the Mother of the Orishas and of all humankind. She was regarded as a life-giver whose compassion was a healing force rescuing the faithful from all trouble.

One of the legends of the enslaved Africans was that Yemajá "allowed" herself to be captured so that she could be brought to the Americas to minister to the people. A connection between the pronunciation of her name, "Yay-ma-Jah" and a familiar slavery personality, Jemima (as in Aunt Jemima), helps us see some interesting connections.

The fictional figure Aunt Jemima has been derided as a negative stereotype of the fat, asexual, "mammy" figure often depicted in Hollywood films such as *Gone With the Wind* or *Pinky*. Various African American actresses such as Ethel Waters and Louise Beavers were called upon to portray a mammy-like character. However, in recent scholarship (Kern-Foxworthy, 1994; Manring, 1998; Saar, 1972) Aunt Jemima has been restored to her more spiritual roots as a caregiver, not of White oppressors but of her own people.

"HOW DID I FIND MY WAY TO COLLEGE?"—JOYCE KING'S EARLY STORY

Whenever I think of the care and healing of Yemajá—our Jemima—I think of Joyce E. King. And I think I know her well enough to say she finds no shame in this image. Indeed, my knowledge of Yemajá comes from my association with Joyce, whom I met in 1979 while I was a graduate student at Stanford University.[1] She was teaching a course for a faculty member who was on leave.

Joyce and I have some interesting similarities in our lives. We were born the same year, started undergraduate school about the same time, and were at the same civil rights protest—the Poor People's Campaign in Washington, D.C.—at the same time. Of course, we did not know each other then and would not come to know each other for another 11 years. We also have some important differences. Joyce was born in a small West Coast town and I was born in a big East Coast city. I have referred to us as "City Mouse and Country Mouse." Of course, anyone who knows that story knows that it ends with the Country Mouse able to accurately discern the dangers of the city and better appreciate country life.

When we met at Stanford, Joyce was an instructor while I was a student. I had attended a Historically Black College while she was an undergraduate at Stanford:[2]

> The question really is how did I find my way to college, to the university that becomes then an opportunity to have other possibilities. I grew up in a small town in central California. My parents were not

educated. I was the second child in my larger extended family to finish high school. I graduated from high school in 1965 and that was just when there were opportunities opening up for Black kids to go to the university. I got a scholarship to go to Stanford. I didn't even know what Stanford University was. I had never heard of it, but one of my elementary school teachers, a Black man I used to baby-sit for and my mom, who was a domestic worker, used to work for when they had parties they sort of mentored me. I also had a scholarship to UCLA, and the only reason I selected Stanford was because they gave me more money. I had no idea that the schools were different, or that one was prestigious or anything like that.

Joyce graduated from Stanford in 1968 with a degree in sociology and entered graduate school in much the way she began her undergraduate studies:

I almost took a job in Oregon [to] work in kind of an Upward Bound kind of setting, but I had also met a professor who was in the college of education and met her through one of my roommates who was getting a master's degree. She [the professor] invited me to apply to graduate school to her program. It was a series of sort of very coincidental happenstance connections that moved me from one level to the other and a developing commitment to make a difference in education, and that pursuit of knowledge led me to the academy.

Joyce completed her PhD in the sociology of education at Stanford University in 1974—10 years before I completed my graduate degree. However, like me, Joyce found out having a PhD from Stanford was no guarantee of securing a tenure track position at a major research institution.

My first professional teaching experience was at Cañada College [a community college] and I was also teaching at Nairobi College [another community college], which was an independent Black institution. Then I went to Mills College. Then Stanford [as a lecturer] and Santa Clara [University].

My own relationship with Joyce King is less a result of taking a course with her (and having her serve as a reader on my qualifying examinations) than our working together in the community. When I met Joyce, we were both mothers who were struggling with the local school system. Instead of continuing to struggle alone, Joyce organized a parents group that we called Parents for Positive Action (PPA).

> I think my personal life informs what I do professionally and what I do professionally has served as a kind of tonic for my personal life. My personal life includes being a mother, it includes being a member of a large extended family that extends even to Africa, and without an intellectual understanding of what is happening to Black people I might have been more victimized by this society.

The parents group of about six to eight parents met regularly at Joyce's home to plan strategies that would force the schools to be more responsive to the educational needs of Black and other children of color. Of course we heard comments about PPA that suggested that we were wasting our time. "Nobody is going to listen to a bunch of Black parents." "We've tried to get them to do right before and they just won't listen." "You're just wasting your time. You can't change things."

The first public activity of PPA was to present the school district with a report card. We wanted the district administration to know that although we were a part of a poor and working-class community, the parents cared as deeply (perhaps even more deeply) as parents in the neighboring affluent school districts. In order to gather information for the report card, PPA organized a forum where local parents were invited to air their grievances. Joyce advised us to avoid too much structure and formality. We would set up chart paper in various portions of a school auditorium and urge parents to go sit with any group. PPA members were there to record their concerns. In one group we stationed a bilingual parent who could translate. We also invited the local newspaper to the forum.

The evening of the forum, more than 75 parents turned out. This was a historic event in this community. And the parents were vocal in expressing their concerns. We heard angry stories, sad stories, and tragic stories about what parents were experiencing as they tried to ensure that their children got a decent education. When we asked many why they decided to attend the forum, they replied that they saw us as an organization from the community, not one that the school district had organized to mollify the concerns of the community. The next day the local newspaper ran a story about the forum. Shortly after that a school board member asked PPA to come to the next school board meeting.

By the time PPA appeared before the school board meeting, group members had summarized the forum comments and indeed created a "report card" on the district. It would be wonderful if I could say that this effort on the part of the parents totally transformed education in the district. It did not. But it inspired in the parent group members a sense of political power that I am not sure any of us felt possible on the eve of neoconservative Reagan era policies.

Working together with Joyce King in Parents for Positive Action demonstrated to me new possibilities for life in the academy. Until that time, I had worried about what kind of person the academy was turning me into and what it would expect of me if I were to join it as a faculty member. For several years we continued to work on community-based efforts to improve the schools. Interestingly, during that time our collaborations were not around our scholarly work. I was learning what it means to use one's intellectual gifts in the service of others.

There are aspects of Joyce King's early childhood that set her on a path designed for service. She is careful to acknowledge that early personal history as crucial in forming her perspectives and social commitments:

> I had a second-grade teacher, a Black teacher in a school where my cousin, who was really like my brother, was expelled from . . . by this teacher. But she chose me to give a *Weekly Reader* subscription over the summer [to] and that was a pivotal event—to have access to a little magazine that you know gave you certain horizons opening up.
>
> I had another elementary school teacher who sort of handpicked a group of us to bring to her home and sort of tutor. She was from Canada with a Scottish background and I remember she made us scones. That's the only, you know, the first time I had ever heard of anything like scones. And all of these events were like a sieve where you're sifting out and at each higher level you get more rarefied.
>
> I had a third-grade teaching . . . I was in a class [that] must have been third- and fourth-grade combination call—with my brother. My brother and I were in a class together with the same teacher and she made it clear that I was the one who was academic and [that] my brother was not bestowed with those kinds of judgments. This same teacher then gave us a load of her discarded furniture and I got a bedroom set that was a little princess-type bedroom set. I mean, there were ways in which being chosen was affirmed with material things and rewards. She gave us her old secondhand stove and so the family benefited. There was a way in which I was groomed, as a 6-year-old I was selected . . .
>
> I had, as a first-grader, this, you know, this thing put upon me, so all the way through elementary school mostly . . . but these two elementary school teachers came to my high school graduation, so they were following me as if, you know, like we know that teachers say, "Well, I'm going to save this one. You know if I can save this one . . . the rest of them I don't know, but at least I can at least save one!"

As I listened to and later read Joyce's interview I was struck by the notion of sponsorship and the role it played in my own life. I located an online definition of the term *sponsored mobility* that read:

> A British term, contrasted with contest mobility, to refer to a method of identifying people at an early age for social advancement and sponsoring, or supporting, them as they prepare for their rise to the top and then guaranteeing them a comfortable position. (http://bitbucket.icaap.org/dict.pl?term=sponsored%2 0Mobility, retrieved on October 22, 2003)

Joyce's story reminded me that I too had benefited from sponsored mobility. I have addressed some aspects of this in earlier writing (Ladson-Billings, 1994). Clearly, I was sponsored. Nothing in my working-class, segregated elementary school background signaled an advanced degree for me in a place like Stanford. My parents had limited opportunities for educational advancement. But, like Joyce, I had teachers who decided I was "worth saving." I do not know what the indicator was—neatness, cleanliness, courtesy, intellect—or some combination of each of them. But I do know that both my fifth-grade teacher and the special reading teacher (for those students who were "advanced") placed me on a track different from that of most of my peers.

My first indication that I was "special" came when I was selected to "skip" the second semester of second grade. No conversation between the teacher and my parents took place. One afternoon the teacher summoned me and told me to turn in my books. "Go upstairs to Mrs. Harris's room. You're going to be in third grade now. I'll miss you, but I know you'll do just fine." I considered that send-off as happenstance. As one of the legions of children in the baby boomer generation, I could see that our class was overcrowded. A new student arrived and I was sent out. But how did she choose me? What was it about me that made me seem to be the "right" student to send?

Throughout elementary school these kinds of selections continued. Today, parents feel it is their duty to regularly intervene in their children's educational lives by petitioning the teacher, completing the homework and project assignments, and demanding special treatment (Anderegg, 2003), but in my elementary school experience, parents parented and teachers taught. My mother and father regarded the teachers as experts and never questioned their teaching (either its content or its substance), their discipline, their opinions, or their decisions. Much like Joyce King's, my movement through elementary school and the perception of who I was as a student were being directed and constructed by a few caring teachers.

"I HAD A PICTURE OF SOMEONE WHO WAS MAKING A DIFFERENCE"—YOUNG, GIFTED, AND BLACK

Although there are similarities between Joyce's early educational life and my own, our collegiate years could not have been more different. She chose Stanford—The Farm—the refuge of the children of the West Coast's richest residents. I chose Morgan State—a historically Black state college that served working-class, first generation-collegians from Baltimore, Washington, and small Maryland towns. As I discussed above, Joyce's decision to go to Stanford was an economic one. Stanford awarded her a more generous scholarship than did UCLA. She also was drawn to Stanford because a favorite Black teacher had a wife who had graduated from Stanford in the 1950s. "They sort of mentored me . . . and so she played a role in sort of giving me the idea that Stanford was a place where you could go to school."

My choice of college was tied to my concern about living in a predominantly White environment—all the time. I attended a well-integrated high school that was almost 50% African American and 50% White, Jewish students. My classes were demanding and intellectually challenging and I enjoyed them. I had both White and Black study partners. However, most of my social activities were with Black teens and that's exactly how I wanted it. I went to school dances, the prom, and my class trip because there were plenty of other Black students there. But often my weekends were comprised of attending house parties, going to the movies, window shopping downtown, and going to church with other Black teenagers. I felt comfortable with my classroom life because I knew that I had another life away from the competition and the lurking tension of race relations that was always just under the surface in the 1960s. I was not going to attend a college where I had to live this 24 hours a day.

When Joyce arrived on Stanford's campus, the young women were wearing white gloves. When I arrived on Morgan's campus, clothing styles were more formal, but they were decidedly Black styles—double-knit dresses, sharkskin suits, and suede and leather jackets. By the time Joyce and I graduated, both campuses had experienced their own Black consciousness revolutions where the bourgeoisie—Black and White—had to come to terms with a new Black identity, one that was politically charged and assertive.

Both Joyce and I had our politics and vision of life in the academy for Black scholars shaped by important African American intellectuals. In her case it was St. Clair Drake, noted anthropologist and author (with Horace Cayton) of the groundbreaking *Black Metropolis* (1945/1993):

> There were critical people in my development. Drake is one. Drake was really a person who was a role model for Black students, and it

was through him that I had a picture of someone in the academy who was making a difference along the lines that I had begun to value. I had had other Black professors but none who inspired me in the direction that I ended up pursuing.

My mentor was Benjamin Quarles, Wisconsin-trained historian, who set an incredibly high standard for his students. Quarles had set out in his work to disprove the prevailing notion that African American scholars could not write an "objective" history of the United States and the role of Blacks in that history. He was successful in his work and produced a number of noted volumes, including *The Negro in the Civil War* (1953/1989) and *The Negro in the Making of America* (1964).

I recall that Dr. Quarles always called us Miss or Mr. in his classes. "Miss Ladson, can you tell us some of the similarities that exist among the various extremist groups?" I was 17-years-old, I didn't know I was entitled to be "Miss Anybody." His formality was not posturing. Dr. Quarles was determined to grant us the respect that we should command in this world. I clearly remember his admonition not to dismiss someone based on race. "Good Negro History can only be done by good historians," he insisted.

"YOU CAN'T TRANSCEND IT, BUT YOU HAVE TO DO MORE THAN JUST SURVIVE IT"—PROFESSIONAL CONNECTIONS

By the time I completed and defended my dissertation (in late 1983), Joyce King had assumed a tenure track position at Santa Clara University where she was an assistant professor and director of teacher education. I was fulfilling a promise I had made to a local school district to work at least a year with them after their generosity in allowing me access for my research.

Joyce was aware that I had completed my dissertation, because I had hired one of the other PPA members to word process the document. As we met for a minicelebration, she asked whether I would consider teaching a class for her program at Santa Clara. I informed her about my commitment to the local school district and she let me know that I could teach the Santa Clara course in the late afternoon or evening. I agreed to give it a try. Working with her at Santa Clara taught me a lot about both the academy and myself:

Being in these institutions is a process of discovery. You have to basically uncover, disclose, vie for . . . to unroll the racism that's embedded in the institution in order to know how best to trans . . . , you can't transcend it—but you have to do more than just survive it. You have to—I felt that I was trying to discover the way in which I could be myself and do what I believed in doing in the face of such racism. That's the process that I experienced over and over again.

After that first quarter of teaching at Santa Clara, Joyce approached me with a more interesting offer. She had received a Kellogg Foundation Fellowship and she needed to negotiate time away from the university. In her typical Yemajá fashion, she thought of a way to benefit me while ensuring the direction of the program. Her brilliant idea was to create a "Coordinator of Teacher Education" who would assist with administering the program and stand in for her during her fellowship-related travels. Not only would I serve as coordinator, but also we were able to identify a number of courses I was well-suited to teach. The program coordination would provide fringe benefits (e.g., health insurance, participation in the retirement fund) and the teaching would allow me to stay current in the field. Although taking the job was a leap of faith (it paid less than the local school district), I was assured by Joyce that it was a good career move and it allowed us to work more closely together toward the issues to which we were both committed.

THOUGHTS ON TEACHER EDUCATION

As a sociologist, Joyce had not planned to venture into teacher education. Her early experiences with teaching helped her recognize some of the major limitations that teaching presented for progressive thinkers:

> I had an early experience in the public schools that convinced me that I convinced me that I could not be a teacher. I was a graduate student, and I ended up doing my research there but I also taught a class [there] and it was a class of kids who had . . . t was like a psychology class it was some kind of an elective and by October [they] had gotten rid of two teachers. It was like the sweat hogs, nobody could teach them, and I went in and taught this class and did, I think, a very good job with the students, but the solutions that I felt the students needed were outside of what was permissible in the school. Kids were having problems with violence. One of my students brought a gun to school! We were trying to make a class that would address their everyday life needs, and the things we did in that class would have been forbidden had the administration known what we were doing.

Joyce's move into teacher education came as a result of an available job. Unlike many people who have the luxury of working in a specific field, many working-class people recognize the need to be flexible in making a living. Joyce and I talked often about how far we had come, status-wise, from the humble beginnings of our parents and family members. However, we were conscious of the need to carry their values with us into every circumstance in which we found ourselves. A favorite saying she shared with me that became an important way for me to think about challenging situations was "Take what you get and make what you want." Her discussion of her work at Santa Clara University is emblematic of that notion:

> Well, I didn't decide to be a teacher educator. I decided to go and apply for a job at Santa Clara University, which happened to be in teacher education. When I had an opportunity to apply for this position at Santa Clara, it wasn't because I had a vision of teacher education. It was more or less [that] I had concerns about what should be happening in schools that is not happening and I was discovering whether or not I could make a contribution that was meaningful to me. So my vision had to incorporate other people who had more background in teacher education and in teaching than I did. I think typically people go into teacher education after they've been teachers, so I didn't have that experience, and I've had a number of positions without having had the prerequisite experiences that one is normally expected to have. But at a Jesuit school like Santa Clara, one of my visions for teacher education was that we need[ed] to deal with the social justice mission of the Catholic Church. You are being educated in a Catholic school. There were encyclicals, there were pronouncements by the Catholic Church that had to do with social justice, and so my initial concern was to infuse the church's own principles in[to] the teacher education program, and that brought me right into conflict with race and class and all the other contradictions that exist . . . because it's fine, you know, on paper, but where is it in the curriculum?

Joyce's serendipitous journey into teacher education did not in any way diminish the significance of her work. Rather than come to teacher education with a narrow focus about how to teach new teachers to employ specific teaching strategies, she came to the job with a broader societal vision.

"THEY'RE NOT BOTHERED BY THE THINGS I'M BOTHERED BY"—BLACK PROFESSIONAL LIFE

I asked all the participants in this study to tell me how they thought their professional lives differed from those of their White colleagues. I asked the question not merely to elicit complaints or cries of inequity but rather to determine whether there was a pattern of differences that might be helpful as we mentor new Black faculty into the profession. What are some of the things they should look out for? How might they prepare themselves for a set of demands different from those placed on their peers? How might we make their road a little easier? At the time that I interviewed Joyce, she was an administrator and her responses reflected a variety of experiences across the academy:

> Well, I'm no longer doing teacher ed in the way I was doing it when I was in Santa Clara. I'm now an administrator and though I have taught students, my students are not just in teacher education. I have people in administration, counseling, a whole bunch of different fields. My colleagues include, then, administrators like myself as well as faculty members. From an administrative point of view I think my colleagues basically don't care about the things that I care about. They're not bothered by the things that I'm bothered by. They're free to accept the mythology of the American Dream that they have arrived. My colleagues are White males for the most part. I do have some colleagues that are Black who basically don't want to rock the boat. Peers of mine who are still in teacher education or doing research—in the academy, not necessarily in administration—I think that they have . . . what would I say . . . I think I have another vantage point from which to view the trenches, the work of the classroom, and I think that sometimes my peers haven't had that vantage point and so they're struggling valiantly to respond to issues that really are embedded in other levels that they don't have access to. If they're struggling to get tenure, they don't see the games that are being played around tenure. If they are struggling with sort of reactionary students, they don't see the way in which the university fails to lead and why, and all those problems that they're having are not just problems that they're having, they're actually institutional problems that shouldn't be happening if the institution was doing what it should do. And that's the perspective that I have because I'm in academic administration and I see that if a chancellor or a president or a provost does take certain positions, then the people who are in the classroom are left with the flotsam and jetsam, trying to do what the institution should be doing for itself.

As a part of asking Joyce to reflect on her professional life, I also wanted her to think about the impact of her work. This question typically is difficult for scholars because one can never be certain of scholarly impact and, at the same time, we seem to worry that talking about the impact and significance of our work can seem self-promoting. Joyce discussed her work in terms of students' responses:

> My students tell me that my writing, my teaching, is life-changing for them. It's as though I have helped them to feel capable of thinking the thoughts that they want to think. It's as though they've gotten courage from my example, and I do make a concerted effort to expose them to a Black intellectual tradition that most of them have not encountered and so I imagine it is rather explosive, but I'm actually doing some interviews with students now about that very question, and so they say that the experience of my class, or reading my work, just opens their mind beyond what they could imagine and in a way that they can't fall into complacency. It's not like a choice or "oh, well, that's interesting, I guess I'll sprinkle a little of that in my work." It's more compelling, so they feel . . . really, they feel the fire of a mission. This is [among] White students, Black students, older, younger [students], and it's so powerful that it's made me more interested in trying to understand it more deeply, what has happened. It has to do with the dynamics of a classroom. It has to do with the community of learning that takes place and the willingness and the courage to ask questions, you know, beyond where they [the students] were with a particular issue.

In addition to impacting students, Joyce's work has also impacted the institution where she has worked. As she discussed what impact she has had on the institution, I was once again reminded why I selected Yemajá as her "alter ego." Rather than choosing to focus on her own career, Joyce exhibits a strong commitment to change things for the good of the whole group—to minister to the people:

> I just taught a class that was designed to impact the institution, not just the three volunteer faculty members working with me. One of the faculty members came to class and gave a talk and she told the students in the class that since I had been at the university, one of the things that I had done was to name things and to give them a language for the experience that they were living in the institution. So what I took that to mean was a kind of truth-telling that one impact that I've had on the institution is that I'm not afraid to say "this is what's happening," and doing that causes the people who make decisions it puts them on notice that someone is going to speak about what is happening, so they then can choose to take action. But the very act of speaking these things makes it more obvious to people makes it less easy to deny and cover up what is happening and what is not happening. This

has to do with hiring Black faculty and it has to do with injustices that students experience. I have [been] opening a pathway to that [institutional] core and all kinds of people come in the office looking for me or looking to bring their problem, to lay it at the door of the institution, and I sometimes wonder what the office might have been like before I came. There were other people who had my position and maybe they did the same thing, I don't know, but the most lasting impact I think will be that people will say this is what she tried to do, or I'm going to try to do what we started that an alternative can and should exist to the status quo and that we who are in the institution can and should you know, we have the ability to create, to craft that alternative. We don't have it handed to us. It's up to us to make it happen and I'm a coalition builder. I work with people across different aspects of the institution, and I really put a lot of stress on teaching, what we teach and how we teach, to elevate the teaching process so the people can see it as a part of institutional change.

Another aspect of professional life is the degree to which young professionals receive mentoring in order to be successful. While sitting at a professional conference luncheon a few years back, I listened as one of my tablemates who is a well-known scholar described how he got his first job. According to the scholar, he studied with an eminent scholar at an elite institution. When he finished his degree, he did not have a job lined up. His adviser picked up the telephone and called a colleague at a major university and told him he really should hire this man. The colleague replied that there were no vacant positions at this time. The adviser told his colleague that he needed to make something available. Apparently, through a series of maneuvers, a position came open and the scholar began a very long and prolific career at that institution. I want to be clear that I think the scholar is one of the field's brightest stars. However, my point is that his access to the academy was facilitated in ways most African American scholars never experience.

During a visit to a colleague's institution, we lounged over a cup of coffee and talked a bit about our careers. She and I were classmates in graduate school and she commented that everyone from our class had landed on his or her feet, but no one had become the "superstar" that I had. First, I was astounded that she would describe me as a superstar. I suggested to her that I had worked really hard and that unlike many of the people she referred to, I had left Stanford with *no* job offers. Had it not been for Joyce King's generous offer to teach a course and later the serendipitous receipt of her fellowship and my availability, I might not have landed an academic job. Second, I reminded my colleague/classmate that perhaps all of the *White* students from our class had landed on their feet, but I could name three Black students who never reaped the benefits of the Stanford experience. One left after the first year, later finished at an East Coast university, and became an administrator. A second works in a middle school library, and a third is teaching elementary school in a low-income school district. One of the things that they all lacked was the scholar who took a sincere interest in their careers and got them started in the academy. I was fortunate enough to have a relationship with Joyce King. Thus I was curious to know who her mentor or mentors were:

> [There was no mentor], not really. I had people who wanted to shape me, but I don't call that mentoring. That's more like some kind of ideological conditioning. They might call it mentoring but I was in a kind of resistance mode. I think Sylvia Wynter would probably have been my closest mentor in the sense of being dedicated to the work, being dedicated to the struggle, but not a mentor in the sense of "this is how you move from one position to another." I don't really have that kind of mentor.

The fact that she did not have a mentor, per se, did not keep Joyce from serving in that role for others. Clearly, I regard her as a mentor and adviser. I trust her counsel implicitly, because I recognize that she has my best interests at heart and she has filled that mentor role with a variety of people:

> I think so, in the sense of everyone that I've worked with. I've tried to say to them, "Where are you headed? What do you want to do? How can we do something together that will advance their work?" In other words, I've seen myself as being a partner in the growth of my colleagues like you. And, I would say Sara, who is a Mexican American woman. I have probably done more mentoring of graduate students and people who were on their way to academe or just getting started in it more so than. . . . Well, I don't know. If I think of several other people, mentoring isn't the right word because I think mentoring has the connotation of "I'm here and now I'm going to help you get where I am" or "follow this path." But my contribution to colleagues has been, I think, more of convening the collaborative, bringing people together who may not know each other, who are not necessarily working together, and then moving the work to another level. [For example] like the publications, collaborating with people like the *Journal of Education* piece that we did. It's like serving as a mentor calling folks together to say that there's something that needs to be done and we all have a piece of it. Let us work together to do that at this moment and

then moving from there to then being a sort of leader of moving the work along, rather than a position. It's not mentoring for positions. It's inspirational, catalytic, calling folks home.

Joyce's perspective on the role of a veteran scholar suggests that rather than attempt to create academic clones (which is a very popular institutional model) where forever people identify you as Professor So-and-So's former student, she worked hard to help young scholars find their own intellectual identities and learn what it means to work in a more collaborative mode.

"IT'S LIKE TRYING TO TURN AN ELEPHANT"—THE IMPACT OF CULTURE ON PROFESSIONAL IDENTITY

One of the premises of this project is that African American teacher educators experience the profession differently from the way their White peers do. This difference is a result of both the external—the institution and the profession—and the internal—the individual's intelligence, temperament, personal qualities, and cultural resources. Thus I asked each participant to reflect on what aspects of African and African American culture were important in his or her professional life. Joyce relayed a deep sense of communal respect and responsibility that she attributes to her cultural background:

Well, my grandmother used to talk about people who were educated fools, so I had an early skepticism of the benefits of education. In other words, it's not just that you go and get an education, but it's what kind of education, so there was a kind of a critical perspective or insight among people in my community that I imbibed that I was aware of. Certainly the values of giving back, of deference for elders, some sense of our own excellence [came from the culture]. Growing up in the church you experienced Black people's excellence from someone performing [a] James Weldon Johnson poem to [singing in] the choir the kind of collective [excellence]. What does being on the usher board represent? There's discipline, there's perfectibility that you're going to learn the precision. There's a sense [that] you represent your group. You have a responsibility, that sense of responsibility that groomed and honed and sharpened [your skills]. It's really a kind of excellence that we expect to participate in that's collective. It's not individual, it is collective. Your excellence is evidenced because you are a part of this cultural community, so that sense of being a part of something, I think, has had a great impact on who I think I am and whom I represent for whom my education is. It's not just for me, it's for that community.

But Joyce also recognized the tensions that arise between the community culture and this new culture that education attempts to recruit us all into. Her thoughts were not unlike those of English scholar John Edgar Wideman (in Kaplan, 2001), who asked:

> Why weren't the novels and poems by Americans of African descent being taught at the university? Why were so few of us attending and almost none of us teaching there ? Why had the training I'd received in the so-called "best" schools alienated me from my particular cultural roots and brainwashed me into believing in some objective, universal, standard brand of culture and art— essentialist, hierarchical classification of knowledge—that doomed people like me to marginality on the campus and worse, consigned the vast majority of us who never reach college to a stigmatized, surplus underclass. (pp. xii–xiii)

Note the similarity in Joyce's expression of her experiences with education:

> But at the same time I think another and not positive aspect of our experience is the alienation that we inherit from the European side of our experience—the alienation that comes from the fear that you're going to go off and be separated—that you're going to educated and then how will you fit in? The sense of how you're belonging . . . your sense of belonging is eroded. The higher up you go in education, the more your natural sense of belonging is chipped away at and so it's that search, that longing for the affirmed whole self, that [notion of] the "talented tenth" . . . you know, there's cost! When you have this fostered mobility . . . when you're the one who is picked out . . . you're the one who is elevated, people think they're saving you, but they can also be damning you at the same time. So then you have to struggle against that separation and that separated-ness that this education system thrives on. They want you to separate yourself and to feel successful. I mean the most well-intentioned teachers think that saving you is separating you.

Joyce's explanation of the cultural conflict that African American scholars may experience is not unlike DuBois's (1903/1953) notion in *The Souls of Black Folks* of "double consciousness" where the African American "ever feels his two-ness . . . two souls, two thoughts two unreconciled strivings (p. 5). In our conversation we explored the conundrum of having a collective consciousness while functioning in institutions that typically foster and reward individualism:

> Well, I understand that the institutions are antithetical to Black people,

but they're also antithetical to White people's humanity. So the [cultural] collision that I experience, I don't experience it just because I'm Black, and I don't experience it personally. I understand that in order to promote what I want to achieve, I can use the institution's own values to promote what it is that I value. The institutions value a Stanford degree so I certainly can remind them that I have a Stanford degree. At the same time I'm taking my office in a different direction. Teaching and being in the classroom I have not had very many teaching experiences when I didn't also have another level of authority. In other words, the 12 years that I spent at Santa Clara, I was Director of Teacher Education so I had a level of authority to buttress the deviation that I was making from the institution's . . . status quo. When I was at Mills [College], I was head of the Department of Ethnic Studies so again I had a way of protecting myself institutionally [on] the institution's own terms. And, this relates to something that a sister in Brazil told me once when we were talking about how she manage[d] to make change in her institution during the military regime before there was a democratic opening, and she said, "Well, you have to have some prestige, of course, first, and then you have to do good work." So the prestige comes in terms of some institutional currency, some type of legitimacy.

Joyce also understood that working in academic institutions and within a profession like teacher education comes with limits, and we discussed the framework in which institutional and programmatic change was possible:

You can't just be, you know, totally "out of the box." I mean, you won't even be there the next day . . . they'll get rid of you . . . you know, you won't even last. But that legitimacy also gives you a little bit of space to maneuver. I don't experience so much of a [cultural] collision as I experience a very wearying, perpetual feeling like trying to turn an elephant. An elephant doesn't have any reason to want to turn and you're just there pushing and tugging and pulling and you know the elephant is just the elephant. It doesn't have any reason to go in another direction or to turn.

JOYCE KING'S SCHOLARLY CONTRIBUTION

While I attempt to craft each of the portraits in this project as separate and unique as the personalities they reflect, it is important to identify the contribution each scholar makes to the field. Once again this choice represents my understanding of the scholar and the way I believe the scholar's work has shaped our thinking about teaching and teacher education. In Joyce King's case, I think immediately of her concept "dysconscious racism" (King, 1991) that gave a name to something many teacher educators were seeing in classrooms with preservice teachers.

According to King (1991), "Dysconsciousness is an uncritical habit of mind (including perceptions, attitudes, assumptions, and beliefs) that justifies inequity and exploitation by accepting the existing order of things as given" (p. 135). This term broke open a new way of thinking about what many of our preservice students were exhibiting. Many of us thought of our students as "unconscious"—that they were unaware of the inequity and oppression that other people experienced. We taught as if providing students with enough information could awaken them to consciousness.

Joyce King helped us understand that our students were not unconscious. They suffered from a distorted consciousness, and that distortion made it almost impossible for them to imagine a different social order. If they could not imagine a different future, how could they inspire students in their classrooms to work toward social change? How could we break the hierarchy and oppression embedded in our current arrangements?

According to Joyce King (1991), our students fail to reflect critically on social inequity because "any serious challenge to the status quo . . . calls [their] racial privilege into question [and] inevitably challenges [their] self identity [as] White people" (p. 135). Further, she argues that many of the multicultural resources we use with preservice teachers "presume a value commitment and readiness for multicultural teaching and antiracist education which many students may lack initially" (p. 142).

Joyce King's analysis of what many teacher educators dedicated to social justice were experiencing in the classroom with our preservice teachers became a powerful rubric for rethinking and reorganizing our practice. Her work also brought us a new way to think about what she terms "diaspora literacy and consciousness" (King, 1992) and "culture-centered knowledge" (King, 1995). Additionally, she has been a leader in challenging the epistemological biases that frame the disciplines informing education. As the driving force behind the Commission on Research in Black Education (CORIBE), an American Educational Research Association initiative, she continues to educate her colleagues and the larger community.

However, I would argue that her more enduring scholarly signature—that offers both theoretical rigor and practical significance—is that of "dysconscious racism." It is impossible to use that term without invoking her scholarship.

"YEAH, THEY WON TODAY, BUT I AM
STILL HERE"—CONCLUDING THOUGHTS

At the end of each interview I asked the participants to share with me what they thought was the most significant aspect of their work thus far and to share a word, slogan, or proverb that expressed the essence of their work. As she did throughout the interview, Joyce reflected on the work of larger struggle rather than a sense of individual accomplishment:

> *Tenacity*, that's the word, and I'm not talking about perseverance but tenacity that . . . that you can stand in the hurricane and you haven't been swept off your feet . . . you haven't lost your mind . . . you can still try to out-think them the next morning . . . you know you can go home defeated one day . . . they got me. But that happened to me one day . . . they got me, they really got me. I thought I was getting someplace and I looked up and you know they had, and I was just so. . . . Three sisters didn't get tenure and promotion and this was on my watch, so I felt very personally accountable that this could happen to three Black women and it happened under my nose and I didn't see it. I mean I was watching so many different things that I . . . I just didn't pay close enough attention. That's how I felt. I felt personally responsible that this had happened and I went home feeling very, very depressed and I just turned on the TV and started watching one of these Disney shows, and it was a story with this brother who played this character part. He was a father trying to get the land that his parents had died slaving on and it was a story about the deceitfulness of White people and the naiveté of Black people and sort of the transition from rural life to when folks went to the city. And, as I looked at this story, it was in the 1930s, I realized [that] things are no different. I'm in the university and he's a skilled worker but we are both totally subject to White authority and power. We don't have any protection against their arbitrary power, so it was just sort of a moment of, "Well, why am I surprised this is happening? Now let me see, what can I do tomorrow? Yeah, they won today, but I am still here . . . and tomorrow I have to go back and deal with this. So . . . when I say tenacity [it's] to be able to say, Yeah, still here!"

We also talked about what Joyce's impact on her students might be, and she expressed the importance of recognizing the gifts that students bring with them to the classroom. Rather than encouraging the arrogance of those who feel they have a teaching "gift" and their gift is the best and only method to pass on, she emphasized her belief in the eduring nurturance of the soul that is the hallmark of Yemajá:

> A student chose to answer the question in terms of my teaching. . . . The student said that I would, without any fear, challenge them and get them to think about things differently. And, this student said that he had been in a very arrogant manner expecting to go out and clone himself as a teacher . . . he basically saw himself reproducing himself. He was a success, so why wouldn't he want to reproduce himself in the students? And he said that I had [pointed out that students] come with their own gifts and that his job is not to reproduce himself but to bring out the best in them, and I thought that was a good way of summarizing what my intention was, because I do find that the White students are quite arrogant in their whiteness and unexamined privilege, and if you can get them to recognize their need to be humble and to recognize the strengths and the values of cultures that are not like theirs, then they are in a better position to learn with the community as they offer what they have to offer.

Finally, Joyce shared with me the saying, or adage, that represents her and her work:

> I guess I would say two things. Something my mother always says, "It can be done!" That was how she always thought about my going to Stanford, you know, "It can be done!" So many of my accomplishments . . . she always says, "Somehow, yes, it can be done!" And then, I would say the way we acknowledge the difference between African world view and European world view, we contrast the Europeans' "I think therefore I am" with "I am because we are."

NOTES

1. Throughout these chapters I refer to the participants by their first names. This signals my close relationship with them, not a lack of respect for their significance and stature in the field.

2. The excerpts of the interviews in this work have been edited for brevity an clarity, but not for content.

FOUR

Carl Grant

High John the Conqueror

Every culture has a tradition of storytelling and within these traditions there are enduring characters. One such character is that of the trickster. In Africa, where many tales have animals as characters to teach moral lessons, there are a variety of tricksters. In stories originating among East, Central, and Southern African peoples as well as those in the western Sudan, the trickster was a hare (Malvasi, 2003). By contrast, the West African trickster was commonly a spider or tortoise. Enslaved Africans preserved these tales in the Americas and added a human trickster.

The trickster tales served an important function in slave communities. They gave slaves a sense of pride and hope. They helped the people to see their dignity and human worth in the midst of the inhumanity of slavery. The trickster tales demonstrated that the weak could conquer the strong. The trickster is an underdog who typically is physically smaller and weaker than his adversary. To compensate for his small stature and limited strength, the trickster relies on his wits and cunning to prevail over enemies. Sometimes the trickster is ruthless and deceptive but he always does what he needs to do to survive and sometimes get what he wants.

For African Americans in slavery the trickster took on an added significance. The character represented the plight of the slaves, and the enemy was always the master or other powerful Whites. According to Malvasi (2003), "The ability of the trickster to outsmart his rivals offered the slaves hope that their master was not all-powerful, and afforded them no small amount of satisfaction to see him beaten and humiliated by one of their own" (from the first paragraph of the Web page).

One of the most important characters in African American trickster tales, High John the Conqueror—sometimes called simply High John or John—is a slave trickster. John was the subject of subversive narrative whose mission was to outsmart his oppressor. In some stories John is able to outwit "Old Master," but in others he is tricked. In Carla Kaplan's (2001) compilation of Zora Neale Hurston's African American folktales, there is an entire section devoted to John and "massa." In one High John tale, John tricks the master into believing that the death of his pig was caused by an illness. Concerned that the illness has infected the entire stock of pigs and will cause his family harm, master gives the pigs to the slaves. The slaves enjoy a feast, knowing that the pigs were not sick and that High John has once again outsmarted the slave master.

John's cunning, to remain both trusted and subversive, makes him a wonderful personality to describe my colleague Carl Grant.

"YOU HAVE TO GET OFF THAT CAMPUS"—MY RELATIONSHIP WITH CARL GRANT

Carl Grant is one of those scholars whom I knew of by reputation long before I knew him personally. Because of my interests in equity, social justice, and multicultural education, it was impossible for me not to come across his name often in the literature. However, I did not come to know Carl personally until Joyce King suggested that we ask him to serve as a discussant on a paper session we were proposing for a major professional conference. My naiveté in dealing with the academy made such a request seem out of my reach. However, I had spent enough time with Joyce to know that she was skillful and forceful at contacting people across the spectrum. She convinced Paulo Freire to speak at "tiny" Santa Clara University. She picked up the phone and got eminent theologian and civil rights leader Vincent Harding to write a foreword for a special journal edition she edited. Contacting Carl Grant was no big deal to Joyce King. As she would say, "What's the worst thing that can happen? He could say no, and we will be no worse off than when we started." However, when she contacted Carl, he listened to the proposal and quickly said yes. His openness and agreement to participate foreshadowed the kind of relationship we would later develop.

After the paper presentation, I did not maintain an ongoing relationship with Carl, but about a year and a half later we were both attending a meeting of the College Board in New York. I arrived at the meeting late, after dropping off my baby girl at my mother's in Philadelphia and attending another meeting in Princeton, New Jersey. I had missed the opening reception and the opportunity to meet the other conference participants. The next morning I joined the group for breakfast and chose a table where Carl Grant was seated, deeply engrossed in a conversation with an African American woman who was an up-and-coming school superintendent. Carl was trying to convince the woman that she should consider a career in the academy. I don't think that Carl noticed that I was at the table at all.

After breakfast when the conference began, I was the second of two morning speakers. My talk described some of the preliminary findings from my work that resulted in *The Dreamkeepers* (Ladson-Billings, 1994). The audience response to my talk was enthusiastic, and I noticed Carl Grant virtually running from the room. I did not know if he had an emergency or if I had said something that offended him. I was wrong on both counts. Carl went to a place just outside of the room but directly in my line of sight from the dais. He began motioning frantically for me to come out to the hall where he was. It was a comical sight. I was busy trying to field audience questions, and here was this icon of multicultural education scholarship furiously beckoning for me to leave. Once the session was officially over, I made my way out to him.

"You have *got* to come to Wisconsin," he began. "I have a stack of resumes on my desk and I will push them all off to get you to Madison." Indeed, I was flattered, but I had lived in a cold climate before and my work at Santa Clara University had finally paid off into an assistant professorship. I wasn't looking for work in the Midwest. "Well, at least come to Wisconsin and give a talk," Carl insisted. I agreed that I would consider that, since it couldn't hurt to have "Lecture at the University of Wisconsin-Madison" listed on my vita. However, I really did not imagine that he would follow through on making a visit happen.

A few months later I received a call from the director of the Wisconsin Center for Educational Research, who asked if I would consider coming to give a talk in the Center's "Visiting Minority Scholars Series." I had no doubt that the impetus for this call came from Carl Grant.

I arrived in Madison on a cold, crisp March day and was quickly overwhelmed by the extensive itinerary that awaited me. I went from visit to visit, meeting any number of scholars, some of whom I had heard of and read about and others who were new to me. I gave my talk on the second afternoon and received a very warm reception with a fair amount of challenging questions to push my thinking. The next day I visited some teacher education classes and continued to meet other scholars. The very last item on my itinerary was dinner with Carl Grant. I appreciated having the opportunity to talk with Carl to thank him for making the visit possible. What I didn't know was that Carl had arranged for me to go to dinner at the home of the then-chancellor, Donna Shalala.

We walked into Chancellor Shalala's home and she greeted me with the words, "Welcome, now what do we have to do to get you here?" I was flabbergasted. "Well, I already have a job," I responded. "That's not the question I asked you," Shalala came back. I had just experienced the force of the no-nonsense administrator. I slowly rebounded with, "Well, I guess I'll have to think about that." Later that evening Carl drove me back to the hotel and suggested that we have a cup of coffee. Many years later I have learned that an invitation from Carl Grant for a "cup of coffee" or "some ice cream" is always an invitation to a very serious discussion.

Over coffee in the hotel bar Carl told me, "Look, these people really want you, but this is not about them. It's not about me. It's about you. You don't have to come here, but you do need to get off that campus you're on. They can never support your work in the way you need. Think about it." Carl's comment that I needed to get off my current campus was some of the best professional advice I have received. It told me that he wasn't trying to get feathers in his cap. He wasn't trying to be a king or queen maker. He didn't see himself as a patron. He had my best interests at heart, and although Carl may not even remember that conversation, I see it as the beginning of a friendship built on trust.

How did I come to associate Carl with High John? In addition to enjoying his wonderful sense of humor, I have had the opportunity to witness Carl in the context of a major research university. He has eschewed the dichotomous roles of accommodationist or antagonist in favor of fully learning the ways of the academy to be able to turn them back on the institution.

"I COME FROM A VERY STRONG FAMILY"

Anyone who knows Carl Grant knows that he is not a shy man. He is confident, witty, and has a spirit of playfulness that many discourage in the academy. After all, we are in a "serious" place doing "serious" work. But Carl seemed determined not to have the academy change him in ways that ran counter to his own sense of self. Where that sense of self emanates from is intriguing. Nobles (1973) argues that African Americans have both a sense of individual self or self-concept and a sense of extended self-concept. This extended self comes from the family, the community, and the culture. In it we see ourselves not merely as individuals who must be concerned solely about personal wants and needs but also as people woven into a broader set of social relations. For Carl, the network was, and is, his family. When I asked each of the scholars about particular people who were instrumental in their professional growth and development, they typically identified one or two people. Carl insisted that it was not just one person. For him, support was a family ethic:

I mean my WHOLE FAMILY. I come from a very strong family . . .
very, very [strong]. I would have to start, you know, [with my] mother,
dad, three brothers. I mean to this day my three brothers are very supportive, and if there's anything going on [that I'm involved in], you will
see them [there]. I mean, they have been to AERA [professional con-
ference] with me, they've been up here [to Madison]. I mean, that's
kind of the way we grew up, so all of them were very, very supportive.

My brothers have always been encouraging, have always said, you
know, "Hey that's [what you're doing] great, great, great . . . keep doing it." That doesn't mean that we don't debate or argue over sports
or get into things like that, but there is truly a respect, understanding,
and a promotion and encouragement of what each other [is] doing,
and we were all in education. [Carl's brothers have been teachers and
school administrators.]

I had some aunts and uncles in both Chicago and in Huntsville,
Alabama, that were very similar, so the whole family [was supportive].
There was really support from both sides of the family, of people let-
ting you know that they cared [about] what you were doing, would
say that was OK, you know.

One bonus of doing research with people whom you know well is
that you have an opportunity to validate the participants' responses. As
a longtime colleague of Carl's, I have had the opportunity to see and meet
his brothers and other family members at a variety of professional settings
where Carl was speaking or being honored. I have seen him reciprocate
this support with his brothers, nieces, and nephews. Now, as he enjoys that
phase of life called grandparenting, he is fully involved in his grandchildren's
education and in securing their futures.

"ONE DAY IN MARSHALL FIELDS"—CARL GRANT
BECOMES A TEACHER

Carl had a vision of himself as a professional early on in his life. He was
raised in Chicago, the third of four boys in a close-knit family of strivers.
He always knew he was going to college. He attended a Historically Black
College, Tennessee State University in Nashville. What changed were his
career goals. Originally, he planned to be a doctor:

My goal was to be a doctor, so I was on my way to medical school
[when] I finished college. But when I was going back for my senior
year of college, my brother said to me, "What will happen if you don't

go to med school?" So I looked at him and said, "What do you mean if I don't go to med school? I'm going to med school. I don't know why I wouldn't go to med school? Why couldn't I go to med school?"

Although he was adamant about a career as a doctor, his brother's questions forced him to think about some other options:

When I went back [to college] for my senior year, something said to me, "Take some education courses," [and] all through my college [career] I had always seen this woman on campus and her name was Dr. Sasser, and when we used to see one another, we used to talk. We used to stop and talk about clothes, you know, because she was usually sharp, I was sharp, and we were just people who liked clothes [laughs], you know, and there was a common interest. So when I decided to go over to the School of Education and walked in the office, there was Dr. Sasser. She looked at me and said, "What are you doing here?" So when I explained [it] to her, she just laughed.

Because Carl's decision to look into education as a field came so late in his college career, he was faced with the challenge of trying to squeeze an incredible number of courses into one year to stay on track to graduate with his class:

[Dr. Sasser] said, "We can do this, but you will probably want to scream before this is over." I wound up taking basically 2 years of courses in a year, so I was going full-time, back-to-back, like practicums and student-teaching together, and taking all of these courses together was fun because I knew her and she knew me and we had a way of talking about things . . . and I mean she held my toe to the line as for what I was supposed to do.

Carl's drive and determination allowed him to graduate on time, but immediately he was faced with a challenge:

When I graduated, I was basically waiting to take off and go and I became very ill. I was in the hospital for 2 years [and] when I came out, [the] doctors basically said that I should not try to go to med school right away. I needed to stay home and get some rest, and so I was staying with my mother and we were downtown one day in Marshall Fields. My mother and I used to shop . . . always go downtown and shop and she [hinted at my becoming a teacher]. I kind of laughed and said, "Oh, no." Mother was always very patient, very wise, and she didn't push me. Later on she said, "You know, if you would teach, you could buy a new car [laughs].

Carl's mother did not so much put the teaching idea into his head as intuit and articulate his unvoiced desire:

> She knew me. We were in Marshall Fields and at that time the Chicago Board of Education was [at] 228 North LaSalle, which was basically about 5 or 6 blocks from Marshall Fields. I ran out the door . . . walked over to the Chicago Board of Education. They had a few little tests you could take. Now this was about 10 in the morning, because Fields used to open at a quarter to 9 and my mother and I would always be standing there when the door open[ed]. When I got in [to the school board], they had my records. Dr. Sasser had already sent my records up there . . . just in case . . . and I went through a kind of medical exam, a 40-minute exam [with] math and a few science questions. Then I went down to what they called "Sub Center" to pick up a sub[stitute]book and the woman there said, "If you get out to the school," which was Crispus Attucks, "by 10:30—no, quarter to 11:00—we will pay you for the whole day." I literally ran out of 228, back over to Fields [and] caught up with [my mother], told her about it, ran back out of Fields, jumped on the subway, made it to Crispus Attucks, ran in there, and I began substitute teaching. That was the beginning of it.

But becoming a teacher really was just the beginning. Carl had a desire to continue to learn, and such learning was not merely instrumental. It was not about earning more credits to climb a salary schedule. He wanted to learn because he was intellectually curious.

"AFRICAN AMERICANS DON'T GET OUT OF THE UNIVERSITY OF CHICAGO"—MOVING ON TO GRADUATE SCHOOL

Although Carl shelved his dream of a career in medicine, he still held on to a vision of himself as an intellectual. What spurred this dream was probably a combination of family support and encouragement, individual drive, and a sociopolitical climate that said it was possible. However, Carl's move to a terminal degree seems to have arisen out of a series of serendipitous circumstances:

> I guess I've always been a person [who] in the summertime, if I was out doing nothing, I was always going to take classes. I was at Chicago

Teachers College taking some literature courses. I used to take the literature courses and I would take the philosophy courses just for fun.

My mother would say I was burning the candle at both ends. I was partying all night, getting up going to class in the morning, but I didn't care about the class, I was just there for the knowledge, not for a grade, just for the knowledge and experience. I remember coming into class and he'd [the instructor] given an exam and he would post the grades [from] the exam. So when I walked into the class, he said the highest mark in the class was some [score] and he asked, "Who has that?" Because he had given out a number, I said, "Oh, that's my number," and he was shocked, principally because it was a class of mainly White students. I think there were one or two [other] African Americans in there. Then he realized it was me, [the one] who came into class with a sailor cap pulled down over his head—[and he] probably wondered why I was there anyway. That happened again, and then he said he wanted to see me one day after class. So he mentioned that [graduate school] to me, which increased my thinking about it. At the time I was teaching at Wadsworth, so the University of Chicago was close and there were some people in the school who were doing a [research] project from the University of Chicago. When I happened to mention to them [that] I wanted to go, they said, "Look, why don't you come to the University of Chicago?" I had always dreamed of going to the University of Chicago, but I also knew [it was difficult] because I had gotten my master's from Loyola and one of the discussions among African American students there was if you [went] to the University of Chicago, you didn't get out. African Americans just would not get out. There was one guy I knew who went there at that time. His name is Bobby Wright, he's no longer alive, who said to me before he went, "Carl, I'm going to go there and I'm going to get out," and he was successful, so he broke that particular mold, but for many who went, you could go in and they would basically keep you forever and you might not get out. So I wanted to go but also did not think it was smart to go [because of the particular anti-Black climate].

So here we have Carl Grant, as a young teacher, enjoying himself as a single Black man in a big city—partying all night yet excelling in classes during the day. However, there was something unfulfilling about where he was in his life and career. The teaching was going well, and before long he was appointed assistant principal of a large school of about 2,200 students. But, once again, someone else encouraged the latent dream that was his:

One day it was a Monday after a Friday that was a payday. So many teachers were out and this was a large school [of] about 2,200 plus. It was a huge school and I was running all over trying to keep the lid on it. I was the only African American administrator in a school that had changed and become African American, so there was just so much to do to deal with that. Bob Crump, a very, very good friend, came in one day. He was in the counseling guidance office. He came in one day about 11 and he mentioned to me that he was coming up to the University of Wisconsin to work on his doctorate, and he said, "Would you be interested in going?" And I said to him, and I laugh about this . . . I said, "Bob, is your car outside?" He looked at me. I said, "[Do] you have gas?" He said, "Yeah." And I said, "Let's get the hell out of here [laughs]." You know, I didn't leave at that moment, [but] by that January I was up here driving back and forth and when I started going to school [I] spent a full day there. I would jump on the expressway [at], oh, 2:15. I would leave my school about 45 minutes early, drive up here for a 4:30 class, get out at 7:00, drive back, get up the next morning and go to work, and I would do this two to three times a week. [I would] come up here on the weekend and use the library and those kinds of things, so that's what got me in.

"IT'S ABOUT LIFE, LIVING, PEOPLE . . . FAIRNESS AND SOCIAL JUSTICE FOR EVERYBODY"

One of the areas of concern examined in this book is the balance the participants strike between their professional lives and their personal lives. I see this as important because many young scholars of color seem baffled by the demands of the professorate. In their quest to earn tenure and promotions, they worry about sacrificing their personal lives. Horror stories abound about the need to plan important relationships and decisions around a tenure clock. More times than I would like, graduate students have asked me, "How do you do it all?" Their sense is that we are drones who do nothing but work, work, work.

As we approached this question about the relationship between the professional and the personal, Carl pointed out that he recognized a necessary overlap between the two:

[They're] like these nice circles [that] would come together. I mean, that's a good question, [as] I said to someone yesterday about a film I wanted to see. They asked me if I had gone to see it; I said, "No, it's too much like work." So most of what of the way I look at the world basically [is] analyzed through my work. That doesn't mean that I can't step away from it or can't relax—that's not to infer that! But it does mean that work in many ways has provided me with knowledge and understanding about things. This knowledge and understanding is broad-based. It's more than about understanding that two and two is four. It's as much about life and living and about people and about the world and about fairness and social justice for everybody. So that permeates my lens, so in many ways that goes together.

Those who know Carl Grant know that like most of the scholars in this project, he is, in mainstream parlance, a workaholic. Of course, African Americans eschew that term and speak about the need to work longer and harder in order to get half as far. That drive and responsibility to go above and beyond the call of duty is a common quality shared among almost all of the African American scholars I have encountered.

Carl is one of the few colleagues I know whom I can call at unseemly hours of the night because I know he will be up working on a paper, editing a book, reading student work, or reviewing a manuscript. His speech is peppered with sentences like, "I was sitting at the computer around 2:00 in the morning when I got this great idea?" or "About 12:30, after I finished watching the game, I decided to try to finish this paper." But he is right when he says, "That doesn't mean I can't step away from it or relax." One of the ways Carl relaxes is through cooking, and he is an excellent cook, trained in a culinary school in Chicago. Here again, we see the pattern of intellectual curiosity leading, not utilitarian function. With his excellent cooking skills, Carl is known for entertaining both colleagues and students. Graduate students know they can get a great meal at Professor Grant's home and Carl understands the need to mentor students, particularly students of color. Carl also opens his home to junior colleagues to encourage them, to get to know them better, and to signal that he is available to lend support. Although it has been about 13 years since the first time my family and I dined at Carl's home, I still remember the meal. He prepared filet mignon, au gratin potatoes, string beans, a tossed salad, homemade croissants, homemade ice cream, and a "made from scratch"[1] German chocolate cake. I can still see my daughter (who was about 5 years old at the time) gobbling up every bit of the meal, and I remember my embarrassment when she turned to Carl and asked, "What kind of meat is this? It's really good." Indeed, that was her first filet mignon. For years after that dinner, whenever we planned a social event at Carl's home my daughter would ask, "Is he making those croissants?" Carl Grant had no trouble laying down his "professor" hat and being a wonderful host.

During my freshman year in college, one of my professors would have students over for dinner in small groups of three or four. During those dinners he got to know us better, but more important, he taught us what it meant to eat in a formal setting. We sat down to a table arrayed with a variety of silverware and a complex (for working-class students like me) place setting. As I grew and matured I realized that his hospitality was not based on showing off or condescension. He was inducting us into a world that many of us did not know but in which we would be likely to find ourselves. Carl is also inducting students into the world of the academy and pointing out that it does slough over into one's personal life.

Carl's easygoing manner with a variety of people in the academy has provided him with an opening to display his special style of humor and sarcasm. Like the trickster with whom I have associated him, Carl says the most irreverent and politically incorrect things to get a rise out of people. To me, on days when I have had the presence of mind to have on a well-coordinated outfit, he says, "I see Chuck [my husband] helped you get dressed again." His comment is designed to get exactly the reaction he gets from me—a look of outrage and denial. Of course, I have joked that his remarks are creating a "hostile work environment" and that I plan to report him for harassment.

Carl would not do this joking with every colleague. He has an uncanny ability to judge people and determine who can and cannot be teased. His joking should not be misconstrued to mean that he does not express anger when appropriate. I am reminded of two occasions where Carl's anger flashed white-hot. The first came when the faculty was discussing the cost of continuing to hire some academic staff whom some faculty members considered unnecessary. The debate went back and forth over whether this was the best use of limited funds. At least one faculty member was adamant that we needed to keep these staff people. Carl had calmly yet persistently questioned their actual value to our program. His question was never addressed in a straightforward manner. In an instant, Carl's voice rose several decibels and he commented, "Nobody fought for X (an African American staff person who was not renewed) like this!" You could have heard the proverbial pin drop in the room.

On a second occasion, the faculty was trying to determine hiring priorities for tenure track positions. This always makes for a tense meeting, because program needs almost always outstrip program resources. Faculty jockey for positions that enhance their work in a kind of enlightened self-interest. Somehow one of the areas that regularly gets new tenure lines was again being considered. Carl began to do a slow burn as the discussion exposed the inequity. Finally, he had had enough and shouted, "Oh, good gracious! When are we going to really say what this is about? You want to give them more because they bring in money. This has nothing to do with the department's priorities!" Quickly, one of the faculty members who was sponsoring this position got offended and got into an "argument" (in the academy, arguments are prized, not fights) with Carl. Carl did not relent. An interesting insight into Carl's personality is that in both instances, I later saw him go to the individual and arrange to meet that person for a "cup of coffee" to talk about what had transpired. I am sure the person saw this as conciliatory; however, I realized that the person was being drawn into "Anasi's[2] web." The next time a contentious issue arose, this colleague would side with Carl because the colleague had come to regard him as "fair and reasonable." Skillful at playing the academic game on the specified terms, Carl almost always has the edge.

CARL GRANT'S SCHOLARLY CONTRIBUTION

I suppose one could write an entire book about Carl Grant's contribution to the field. He, along with James Banks, Geneva Gay, and Carlos Cortez, is one of the founders of what we think of as multicultural education. His work extends over a 30-year period, and many young scholars in this field owe a debt of gratitude to Carl Grant for opening it to them. As I have with all of the participants in this project, I am limiting my discussion of Carl's scholarly work to some portion of his impact on teacher education.

In 1987 Carl (along with Christine Sleeter) published an article in the *Harvard Educational Review* entitled "An Analysis of Multicultural Education in the U.S.A." This article represented the first comprehensive look at the field and the literature that defined it. Sleeter and Grant (1987) found that multicultural education was a diffuse field that was characterized by five primary orientations—teaching the exceptional and culturally different, single group studies, human relations, multicultural education, and education that is multicultural and social reconstructionist (EMC-SR). This last category, EMC-SR, represents Carl's major contribution to the field. Although he and coauthor Christine Sleeter could not find much literature that exemplified this conception of multicultural education, their work created a framework for assessing the quality of multicultural education programs in schools throughout the nation. Soon after the publication of this article, Grant and Sleeter (2003) published *Turning on Learning,* now in its third edition, and *Making Choices for Multicultural Education: Five Approaches to Race, Class, and Gender* (Sleeter & Grant, 2003), now in its fourth edition. Both books help teacher educators translate the literature of multicultural education and create appropriate classroom lessons that address issues of difference, equity, and social justice.

In addition to producing a long list of scholarly publications in multicultural education, Carl Grant must be acknowledged for his work in bringing the National Association of Multicultural Education (NAME) to national prominence. As president of NAME from 1994 to 1999, Carl brought the association added legitimacy in the scholarly community. In its early years practitioners acknowledged NAME and its importance to their work. However, under Carl's leadership NAME began to draw interest from a wider array of scholars and became an important venue for new scholars in the field to meet and network with both senior scholars and other new scholars.

Such association work rarely merits reward in major research institutions. Carl understood his work in NAME as more than a personal recompense. He realized that the field had to have a voice that was unrestrained by the boundaries of traditional associations who place multicultural education into special interest groups and task force categories. By creating a home for scholars and practitioners in multicultural education, Carl Grant helped to build the kind of political momentum that the field needs to be able to "speak truth to power." During his leadership NAME opened its Washington, D.C. office and began publishing its conference proceedings. Carl served as editor of the proceedings and brokered the deal with the publisher.

It is not surprising to me that Carl Grant would be known for institution building. Although he has a sincere love of scholarship, his ability to connect with people makes him special. Helping to nurture a living, breathing organization like NAME distinguishes him from many scholars. Instead of merely residing in the Big House, through his work Carl provides a way into the house in hopes that enough people will gain access and transform it.

"RACISM IS STILL A PART OF THE EXPERIENCE"

One of the arguments I have advanced in this project is that African American teacher educators are not immune to the dailyness of racism, despite their education, training, and accomplishments as scholars. I do not mean to suggest that their experience in the academy is about only race and racism. Rather, I am arguing that race and racism do not evaporate because one spends his or her time with "educated," "enlightened," or "liberal" people. Racism is a part of the fabric of life in the United States (Bell, 1992). It is not only the overt affronts and assaults on the person but also the subtle and nagging doubts that are expressed in countless ways as we attempt to go about our work. "Is he really qualified?" "Can we allow her that much responsibility?" "I am amazed at how intelligent (articulate, creative, etc.) he is." Questions about one's competence and "fit" are always in play in a racialized society. It is no different in the academy. Carl's entire career in the academy has been at the University of Wisconsin-Madison. He is probably the first African American to receive tenure in its School of Education.[3] He has witnessed a lot over his three decades at the university. For many of those years he was the only African American faculty member in a large department. But he is the first to admit that there have been improvements:

> It's [the institution] got increasingly better over the years. I think once people see you intend to hang on, and not quit, and be there, and will demand respect and give respect . . . and do what's asked . . . I mean, adhere to what they call scholarship, service, and teaching, then they basically leave you alone. So then you can be at peace and they can be at peace. So that's what I mean basically [by] become increasingly [better]. That doesn't mean that institutional racism and everyday racism have not been a part of the experience, because it has been a part of the experience. And as I listen to graduate students, it's still a part of the experience.

Although he recognizes the racism that exists in the academy, Carl continues to have hope for the future and believes the field of teacher education can be moved closer to his ideals of equity and social justice. The remarkable thing about Carl Grant is that he has been championing issues of diversity and multiculturalism throughout his entire career, even when they were not particularly popular ideas. He earned tenure researching and writing about these issues during a time when there would have been few senior scholars to serve as expert reviewers of such work. The pioneering aspect of Carl's work is truly undervalued.

> [I would] say I have an optimistic vision, but an optimistic vision by realizing that things are so political. As much as we say we are concerned about children, we're [really] concerned about how do we do it without ruffling the feathers? I mean, because the division of teacher ed[ucation] I'm speaking of relates to those who are marginalized—all right, because I think it has to be looked at for everybody but, while looking at it [for] everybody, you would be foolish [not to] pay attention to those who are in need of issues related to social justice, to multicultural education—those who have been disenfranchised. So teacher education needs to focus what we're doing [to meet the needs of] the marginalized.

In addition to getting his response on institutional issues, I wanted to know how Carl perceived his experience as a colleague on a faculty in which he was the only African American for so many years. Carl indicated that one of the major issues is that as the only African American in the department, he often had no one to talk to about his experiences. He felt that students of color in the department have a similar experience. "The few people who *do* get here who are of color—and any who are marginalized—are often looking for someone who they believe is understanding to talk with." Carl's recognition of that loneliness and isolation is what prompts him to so regularly open his home to students of color. A few years ago Carl came into my office and said, "We need to have some sort of social event for the students of color." Ever the trickster, he added, "and we need to have it at your house!" I understood that as a new grandfather he did not have the flexibility that I did in my home, but I clearly sensed another Carl Grant: "Gotcha!" We invited students throughout the School of Education, not just from our department, and had a gathering of about 50 students. It was a wonderful evening and the students said over and over how much they appreciated being invited and having the opportunity to talk with other graduate students of color, some of whom they had not yet met. The following year the students began asking, "When are we having our 'Students of Color' party?" Carl and I organized another party, this time at his home. Carl was a wonderful, gracious host and an emblem of the safe haven that students of color seek on university campuses.

Although Carl demonstrates a warm and inviting presence on the campus, it is not something that he learned from the academy. When I asked about his own experience with being mentored as a junior faculty member, he had few examples of faculty reaching out to cultivate his career. He could not think of very many individuals who extended a sincere helping hand to ensure that he was successful as a professor:

> Not really I have some people I would say that no one was assigned to me as a mentor. When I had questions about how the system worked, there were one or two people that I felt very comfortable in going to ask about [things]. I wasn't talked to about how to publish, how to do this, where to send an article and I mean, oh no, no, no, no, oh good gracious, no, you know I mean, oh wow, no!
>
> In many ways what I've tried to do is to demystify the whole process [the publication and tenure process] and, in part, let people know the "emperor has no clothes," you know, and once we begin to understand that, then you can begin to deal with it.

It is a testament to Carl's decision to be a "different" kind of faculty member that throughout our interview, which took place in his office, his phone rang often and on several occasions the caller was a junior faculty member (from outside of Carl's institution) asking for advice. Carl was generous with his time and supportive, but he was also direct. "What do you want to do?" is the question he asked in a booming voice. "This thing is about you and you have to know what you want to do." This no-nonsense approach rarely appears in the academy. People like to talk in circles and equivocate. With Carl, communication is direct without being harsh, to the point without being terse, honest without being mean-spirited.

"THE FIRST PERSON YOU PAY IS YOURSELF"

As we wrapped up our interview, I asked Carl to think about how African American culture influenced his work. I was not surprised to hear him relate his response back to his family:

> I was raised in an African American home that basically had a strength. I knew about racism at a very early age. I also knew about sexism in conversations with my mother. My mother, who had four boys, started early in teaching us how to do everything [like cook, clean, iron] and talked to us about relationships and respect for women. So part of what I do today, that started years and years ago; so the culture [that I pull on] is a family bond. And within that [I developed] self-confidence. I don't intimidate [easily]. You know I just don't. I mean you can come in here and see me and I'm going to look [right] at you. I mean you can be [President] Clinton, you can be whoever you want to be, you know unless you've got a gun up to my head, and I'll tell you to go to hell in a minute.
>
> I guess one thing my mother told me years ago, the first person you pay is yourself, so if that rainy day [when you lose your job] comes and you have to leave something that is not in your best interest, you are able. You don't have to stay there and hurt yourself emotionally, physically. But you have enough to hold you during that rainy day while you're making that transition and that's a source of comfort, you know.

The significance of Carl's comments here is that he has spent his entire academic career at one university, yet he has no reservations about leaving it if things were to become intolerable. Unlike many of our colleagues whose entire identity is tied to their institution, Carl is able to disentangle his own interests from those of the institution. He has institutional loyalty but not the kind of loyalty that is self-destructive. Carl's ability to separate his identity from that of the institution is part of what it means to be an African American scholar who functions "beyond the Big House." It requires a different response from the one described by Malcolm X in a speech just a few weeks before his assassination.

Malcolm X (1965, February 4) was quoted as saying that some African Americans are so captivated by the lifestyle and culture of the dominant group that they work against their own self-interests. In a speech to some young civil rights workers in Selma, Alabama, entitled "The House Negro and the Field Negro," he said the following:

> There were two kinds of Negroes. There was that old house Negro and the field Negro. And the house Negro always looked out for his master. When the field Negroes got too much out of line, he held them back in check. He put 'em back on the plantation.
>
> The house Negro could afford to do that because he lived better than the field Negro. He ate better, he dressed better, and he lived in a better house. He lived right up next to his master—in the attic or the basement. He ate the same food his master ate and wore his same clothes. And he could talk just like his master—good diction. And he loved his master more than his master loved himself. That's why he didn't want his master hurt.
>
> If the master got sick, he'd say, "What's the matter, boss, we sick?" [Laughter] When the master's house caught afire, he'd try and put the fire out. He didn't want his master's house burned. He never wanted his master's property threatened. And he was more defensive of it than the master was. That was the house Negro.

As I listened to Carl, I was also reminded of a story from Indian philosophy by Idries Shah (1971) in *The Wisdom of the Idiots*. One of the parables is the story of a man who becomes so captivated by a woman that he cannot take his eyes or his mind off her. When he does look away, he sees her everywhere he looks. One day while sitting on a riverbank, he glances down into the water and although what he sees is his reflection, he once again thinks he sees the woman who is the object of his affection. Excited by what he perceives as her nearness, he leans over, like Narcissus, to kiss her. Again like Narcissus, he is unable to swim and drowns in his pursuit of his object of love.

This story serves to remind African American scholars that they cannot become so enamored of the institution and/or life in the academy that they can no longer see themselves. The institution and academy life can be both deceptive and illusive and get in the way of work that better serves the interest of people like them.

Carl Grant may indeed be a kind of trickster. He is smart, clever, and wise about life and the academy. But he is not a house Negro. His solid grounding in his family placed him on a clear path to personal and cultural uplift. When I asked him what he saw as the most significant aspect of his work, he was succinct and direct: " I try to be fair and treat everybody straight up, and also I try to offer people a few things to think about, you know . . . no solutions, but things to [cause them] to stop and pause about it for a few minutes."

NOTES

1. Among African Americans it is indeed a high honor when someone makes you a "scratch" cake as opposed to a "box" (as in Duncan Hines or Pillsbury) cake.

2. Anasi is a spider trickster in West African folktales.

3. We have had this conversation several times. The university and the school have not supplied any data regarding the first African American to receive tenure in the School of Education, but we cannot find a record of any scholar before Carl.

FIVE

Jacqueline Jordan Irvine

Harriet Tubman

Given the increased emphasis on multicultural education and content integration (J. A. Banks, 2004), it is the rare school student who has not heard of Harriet Tubman. A quick perusal of the Amazon.com Web site indicates that there are more that 1,100 titles related to Harriet Tubman—most of them books for children and young adults. However, when I first entered college and learned that the freshman women's dormitory was named Tubman Hall, I was surprised to learn that the name did not register with many of my classmates. I had the advantage of having had a fifth-grade teacher who insisted that we know Black History, so the names adorning the campus buildings and landmarks (Frederick Douglass, Sojourner Truth, Benjamin Banneker) were familiar to me.

Harriet Tubman's story is familiar to many. Born into slavery in about 1820, in Dorchester County, Maryland, Araminta Ross was named for both of her parents. She was described as an enslaved person of "purely African Ancestry" (*Timeline*, n. d.). At the age of 11 she was no longer known by her "basket name," Araminta, and was called Harriet. At the age of 12 Harriet Ross suffered a serious injury to her head, inflicted by a White overseer for refusing to assist in tying up an African American man who had attempted to escape.

In 1844 Harriet married John Tubman, a free African American who naively believed that marriage to him would protect Harriet from the cruelty and whims of a slave master. Harriet knew better and began plotting her escape to freedom. Five years later she left John Tubman and, with the directions from a White abolitionist, made her way to her first house on the road to freedom. Once she arrived in Philadelphia, she got a job and began saving her money in order to help free other enslaved people. She met William Still, a freeborn Black, and became active in the antislavery movement. It was her association with Still and the Philadelphia Anti-Slavery Society that helped her understand the workings of the Underground Railroad. In 1850, Harriet helped her first enslaved Africans escape to the North when she sent for her sister's family in Cambridge, Maryland, to board a boat that sailed up the Chesapeake Bay to Bodkin's Point. There Harriet met them and guided them from safehouse to safehouse in Pennsylvania until they reached Philadelphia.

In September of 1850 Harriet became an official conductor of the Underground Railroad, which meant that she had learned all of the routes to free territory and had taken an oath of secrecy regarding all information pertaining to the Underground Railroad. She also made another trip South to rescue her brother James and other enslaved African Americans. In the same year that she became an Underground Railroad conductor, the Fugitive Slave Act was passed. This made it illegal for any citizen to assist an escaped slave and required escaped slaves to be apprehended, turned in to authorities, and returned to the owner. This act forced the workers on the Underground Railroad to change their destination from the "North" of the United States to Canada. Because of her role as a successful conductor on the Underground Railroad, Harriet Tubman had a bounty of $40,000 placed on her head. The state of Maryland alone offered a $12,000 reward for her capture. Using the 2004 Consumer Price Index, the amount of money offered to capture Harriet Tubman would be $785,542 and $235,663, respectively.

Harriet's third trip was in September 1851 when she went to get her husband, but by this time John Tubman had remarried and did not want to leave. When she left and arrived at the home of station master Thomas Garrett, she found that there were many runaways who needed help. Harriet got them to Frederick Douglass's home where they remained until he collected enough money to finance their trip to Canada. Until 1857 Harriet lived and worked in St. Catherines, Ontario, where she saved her money in order to help finance her work as an Underground Railroad conductor. Between 1852 and 1857 Harriet Tubman made 11 trips between Maryland and Canada. Her most famous trip involved an enslaved African American who grew fearful and wanted to turn back. Tubman understood the danger of allowing someone who had begun this journey to return. Such a person could be tortured and coerced to reveal important information about the escape route and the abolitionist networks. Tubman reportedly pointed a gun at the man's head and said, "Dead folks tell no tales." Needless to say, he changed his mind and continued on to freedom.

In 1857 Tubman set out to rescue her elderly father, Ben Ross. This was one of her most daring trips in that she bought a train ticket and traveled in broad daylight, bought a horse and buggy in Caroline County, Maryland, and took her parents to fellow abolitionist Thomas Garrett, who assisted in their safe passage to Canada.

Tubman's career as an Underground Railroad conductor ended by late 1860. However, she made one last rescue trip that December where she brought seven people to freedom in Canada. During her tenure as a conductor to freedom Harriet Tubman made 19 trips to the South and rescued more than 300 people. It is no wonder that she became known as the "Moses" of her people.

During the Civil War, Tubman served as a soldier, a spy, and a nurse. Although she won admiration from the military, she did not receive a government pension for more than 30 years. While guiding a group of Black soldiers in South Carolina, she met Nelson Davis, who later became her husband.

Tubman was known and revered by some of the most influential people of the antislavery movement—Frederick Douglass, John Brown, Jermain Loguen, and Gerrit Smith. During the mid-1850s she met U.S. Senator and former New York State Governor William H. Seward and his wife, Frances. Mrs. Seward provided a home for one of Tubman's nieces, Margaret, after Tubman had helped her escape from slavery in Maryland. In 1857, the Sewards provided a home for Tubman where she lived for a time with her parents.

At the close of the Civil War Tubman returned to Auburn, New York, and continued to be involved with the fight for social justice, particularly on behalf of women's rights. In 1908 she built a home for the aged and indigent where she worked as long as she could and was later cared for herself until her death in 1913.

The mainstream discourse on Harriet Tubman frames her as an American hero and freedom fighter but fails to acknowledge her powerful role as a resistance leader who challenged the status quo and the fundamental beliefs that shaped the nation. Recent books on George Washington (Wiencek, 2003) and Thomas Jefferson (Wills, 2003) indicate that both men were not merely captives of their times. They knew that slavery was wrong and yet they perpetuated it for their own benefit. Washington grew up in close association with enslaved Africans and reportedly had some Black relatives through his relationship with the Custis family, the family of his wife, Martha. Jefferson benefited from the way the three-fifths compromise gave the South inordinate representation in Congress and electoral votes. What Harriet Tubman represents is an individual who was unafraid to challenge the status quo and resist the injustice that was perpetrated on people of African descent and women.

Tubman's resistance is reminiscent of Patricia Hill Collins's (1998) notion of "visionary pragmatism," which emphasizes "the necessity to link caring, theoretical vision with informed, practical struggle" (p. 188). Tubman was not content to free herself, or to free enslaved Africans. She was attempting to free a nation that had shackled itself to an inhumane and violent system that could only destroy people and distort their perspective. Thus Tubman's life and work have come to symbolize not only physical courage but also moral activism.

"DON'T MAKE ME KILL THAT WOMAN"—MY RELATIONSHIP WITH JACQUELINE JORDAN IRVINE

On the surface, Jacqueline Jordan Irvine has little in common with Harriet Tubman. Jackie grew up in the security and comfort of a working-class family that knew it would send its children to college. Jackie's major work growing up was to study and do well in school. Nothing in her early experiences paralleled the hardship and poverty that Tubman endured. Yet I believe there are a variety of reasons that make Harriet Tubman an appropriate personality to associate with Jacqueline Jordan Irvine. The more obvious reasons are Jackie's courage, strength, and sense of purpose. However, the reason that speaks most forcefully to me is the similarity of their boldness.

I first met Jackie Irvine in 1985 at a professional conference. Joyce King and I, along with some other Black women teachers, were presenting a paper. Our paper session was relegated to an early Saturday morning time slot where we were assigned a table in the corner of a very large auditorium and the only person to show up for the session was Jackie Irvine. To my surprise she stayed throughout the session and offered us some constructive suggestions for submitting proposals for subsequent conferences.

A few months later I attended a conference in Monterey, California, where Jackie was one of the plenary speakers. This was the first time I heard her discuss her concept of "cultural synchronization" (Irvine, 1990). Although both of our meetings at professional conferences were cordial, I do not think I really got to know Jackie until a year or so later at another professional meeting. In the midst of a business meeting, a woman nominated Jackie for an office—one of those hard-work, little-gratitude tasks that every organization needs done. Jackie politely and graciously declined and shortly after got up to leave the meeting. I was sitting in the very rear of the room because I had another meeting to attend and wanted to be sure I could slip out of the room unnoticed. As she approached the exit, Jackie and I exchanged smiles and she bent down to whisper in my ear, "Don't make me kill that woman! I told her not to nominate me for that position."

At that moment, I doubled over in suppressed laughter. Jackie revealed her "round the way" (as we referred to neighborhood friends) personality. Despite her position in the academy, she was "just another sister" and not afraid to let me know that. Her comment reminded me of Harriet Tubman's "Dead folks tell no tales." I wonder whether the woman who made the nomination realized her mistake.

From that moment on, I knew I could deal with Jackie in an open and honest way without the pretense or trappings of the academy. Her primary mission has been the education of our children, and she believes that doing an excellent job of preparing teachers is one of the more powerful ways of ensuring that education.

"THOSE GOOD-LOOKING BLACK WOMEN"—JACKIE IRVINE'S ROAD TO THE ACADEMY

When Jackie and I began our conversation about how she arrived at the academy, I was struck by her self-assurance about the academy as the place for her. In my own journey it never occurred to me that I could end up as a college professor—even when I was a graduate student. Somehow I imagined that I would earn my degree and get a job working in a large urban school district as a curriculum developer or perhaps a curriculum consultant. Jackie's perspective was very different from mine:

> I was looking through my high school yearbook and saw that I said in 1964, when I graduated from high school, that I wanted to be a professor. I had forgotten that, but I grew up about 40 miles from Tuskegee Institute and all my life I had seen these good-looking Black women with briefcases teaching in the academy, and I just figured that's something I really wanted to do. So I knew very early on that the academy and that life, intellectual life, always interested me.

Jackie grew up in a segregated Black community where she saw a variety of Black professionals even though her own parents were not professionals. However, they had high aspirations for their children and supported Jackie and her sisters in their quests to be college educated:

> My daddy did 30 years in the military and my mother [was] a teacher's aide. Both finished high school and neither one of them ever went to college and so my sisters and I [are] all first-generation college. We all went to Howard, but it's interesting though . . . you know, I can't remember a time when in the segregated community in Alabama where

I grew up that people didn't assume that we were going to college. No one knew how we were going to get there, who was going to pay for it, but [we were going].

Jackie's experience of the uncertainty of how her family would be able to afford college was not unlike my own experience. My mother sent me to college with just enough money for one semester and indicated that we would have to "pray our way through this." In the mid-1960s few Black students had college funds that guaranteed that resources would be available to pay for a college education. From this 21st-century vantage point I am so taken by how poor my family was. My brother was in college because of the G.I. Bill and a variety of part-time jobs. I was attending an out-of-state Historically Black College that had tuition of less than $200 a semester. My room and board was less than $100 a month. Yet the amount seemed astronomical to my laborer father and clerk mother. My mother was counting on cashing my brother's endowment insurance policy of $500 in a year or so, but that first year required quite a bit of creative financing.

Jackie's situation is more remarkable because at one point all three of the sisters were attending Howard University at the same time. I was interested in what made her choose Howard when she had grown up so close to Tuskegee:

I think actually it was because we had an aunt, my mother's sister, [who] lived in D.C. and Howard had the reputation in the South of being "the capstone" and so my parents wanted us to go to the best school they could possibly send us to, so it was a combination of scholarships and some loan money. We all managed to get through Howard and that's stayed a family tradition. One of my sisters teaches at Howard. It's a tradition.

Like Carl Grant's, Jackie Irvine's parents played a powerful role in her perspective on education and her decision to be an educator. And, like Joyce King, Jackie had a caring teacher who assisted and sponsored her toward her goal:

When we were little, although we didn't have a lot of money, my mother had a lot of middle-class values. [She'd take us to the library—on the military base, since there was no public library for Black children] and she would always have a car full of other people's children, and I used to say, "Mother, why do all these children have to go with us?" And she said, "I just can't take you-all. I've got to take all these children and maybe when you get back you-all [will] have somebody to talk about [the books] with.

I would say a number of Black women have made a significant difference in my life. One of them was in my senior year [of high school]. Although I went to Catholic schools most of my life, my senior year I went to public school because the Catholic school closed and there was this Black woman who taught social studies. You know, the kind of Black woman who comes in sharp with the spike-heeled shoes and then puts her house shoes on [laughs]. She came in sharp as a tack, put her house shoes on, and she was the one I think that used to let me know she thought I had something really special and would take me to social studies fairs. I used to travel with her all over Georgia to social studies conventions . . . and in terms of high expectations, she exemplified that.

The kind of early mentorship described above was also apparent during Jackie's university experience and during the early stages of her career:

When I went to Howard [University], there again were these African American professors that made a tremendous difference in my life. One is the [person] I always acknowledge as sparking [my interest in the academy and intellectual work]. That's Faustine Jones-Wilson. Faustine made all the difference in my life. She's now Professor Emeritus [and] former editor of the *Journal of Negro Education,* and she just helped me a great deal through both professional and personal issues I was having. When I graduated from Howard I was just 20 years old and I didn't know what I wanted to do, and Faustine has always been there. By the way, she still is my mentor, and after all these years we still have contact.

The other [person] is Anne Pruitt [Logan] who was at Ohio State for a while. I worked for her husband in Cleveland for about 2 years and Anne Pruitt is also a mentor. They were very critical in my development and I've always emulated and modeled [them]. I can identify those women [as critical].

As I listened to Jackie's story, I once again was struck by the parallels between her experience and my own. As with Joyce King, Jacqueline Irvine and I were in undergraduate school at the same time. Jackie was attending school just 40 miles south of me, and I probably spent half of my college weekends in Washington, D.C., attending parties, going to games, and just hanging out. But, of course, our paths never crossed, even though we seemed to be traveling the same road. What was different about her in comparison to me was her ability to have the good sense to follow the direction of trusted mentors. I, too, graduated from undergraduate school at age 20, and although there were caring and helpful professors who offered useful advice, I was so focused on the social and political upheaval of the times that I could not (or would not) focus on jobs and career. I had a revolution to help foment. Martin Luther King, Jr., was assassinated the month before my graduation. Baltimore and Washington, D.C., erupted into riots and were under police-enforced curfews. At that moment in time, academic life seemed self-indulgent and futile.

"WHAT ABOUT THE OTHER CHILDREN?"—FOCUSING ON URBAN EDUCATION

Although I was headed off to the revolution, my parents helped me understand that they would not be financing my liberation work. I needed to eat, have a place to stay, and pay my bills (which included a fair amount of student loans), and in the midst of a severe teaching shortage, it was not difficult for me to get a job. However, once in the classroom I recognized that there was plenty of political struggle in which to engage right there.

Jackie Irvine graduated from Howard University with a degree in political science and secondary education and taught briefly in the public schools of the District of Columbia. During the time she was teaching she was also completing a master's program at Howard University. She had known for some time that she wanted to teach at the college level and after moving to Cleveland, where her husband was finishing a PhD at Case Western Reserve, the Irvines moved to Atlanta. Jackie enrolled in a doctoral program at Georgia State University. Her decision to pursue an academic career focused on urban education was validated by her public school teaching experience:

> So my motivation for teaching and I think my research is motivated by what I see in public schools with the children who look like me. They remind me of my own child. They don't do well in school and so I figured that the little that I could possibly do to make a difference in their lives is what I should dedicate my research and my teaching to.

She reiterated this theme later in our conversation.

> My interest in urban education and educating the African American children, I guess like many of us, began when my own child entered public school and all the things I had read about, at least with other people's children, I was seeing happen to my own child. [I] had to explain to her about racism and why some children are selected and

some children are not selected, trying to explain to her that the teacher is to be respected but sometimes teachers make mistakes, and that was very difficult for me. And, also to see the kind of low expectations that they often ascribed to my own child and how quickly they changed once they found out that she was the child of two college professors. Once they figured out that I was going to be on the case every day, all day, they changed, and I was always concerned about the children whose parents weren't as strong an advocate . . . why they had to depend on the advocacy of just two, you know, politically astute parents. What about the other children? It just tears your heart apart really about all those children left behind. That's why I figured that maybe I would try to make a difference in more than just my child.

Jackie's comments are familiar to me and reflect the kinds of things I hear from African American parents in schools, churches, and social organizations—an emphasis on the collective. We cannot be so consumed with our own cares that we lose sight of the larger issues impacting our children and ultimately the society.

"I ONLY HAD A BRIEF WINDOW WHEN I WASN'T TAKING CARE OF SOMEBODY"—SCHOLAR AS CARE-GIVER

Like many members of the baby-boom generation, Jackie finds herself in the position of having completed child rearing and being plunged into the reality of providing care for elderly parents. In addition to caring for family, academics also care for the next generation of scholars. Although there is nothing unique about this caregiving, Black scholars often refer to the added expectations that students (and sometimes colleagues) place on them to "take care of things" and be nurturing. As I talked with the scholars in this project, I heard several stories about helping students with personal issues (e.g., financial problems, family challenges, health concerns) along with advising them about their intellectual work and careers.

Jackie has had the advantage of being married to an academic having two siblings out of her three who also are academics. This family connection to scholarship has helped to blur the lines between her personal and professional lives:

I have a hard time making a distinction [between personal and professional]. I think a good part of it is that I enjoy what I'm doing so much that I don't make a distinction between work and play. As I get older, I'm trying to make a distinction between professional and personal, but I have a hard time doing that. I work at home and I work at work, so that blurs the distinction greatly for me.

[It's not difficult] in my life, particularly because my husband is an academic and we both are doing the same thing. For the last 30 years we've both talked about our work at home a lot. I read what he reads. He reads what I read. Two of my sisters are academics (and my older sister is retired), but when the academic sisters get together we're always talking (about) academia. But one of the things that has changed, forcing me to see things differently, is my [parents' illness] and so I have had to learn [to] never regret any minute I spend with my parents who live 100 miles from my house. This has changed my personal life tremendously. I'm now back into . . . I only had a brief window when I wasn't taking care of somebody.

[Because I'm caring for my parents], I'm doing less writing than I've done in the past, but I don't regret it. This is what I have to do, but I don't think, as far as encouraging other African American young women to come into the profession, [that] this is a big problem. I think they say we work too hard, that we don't have another life, and I don't. I'm trying to model a more balanced life which is extremely difficult, because once you get on that tenure track, you don't know any other way to behave. You can't go re-socialize yourself in a different way, and the demands on your time escalate.

I don't regret doing this, but [in] my 20 years as a professor, the Black students—undergraduate and graduate—no matter who their adviser is, they always come to the Black faculty. They're always in your office for personal as well as professional problems. And I don't regret doing it, but it's just part of what it is we all have to do.

Jackie's acknowledgment that much of a life of service is about care resonated with me. My own mother is in need of full-time care, as was my father before his death. This mode of operating is fairly alien in the academy, and when students find a faculty member who extends such care, they let their peers know about it. Soon long lines start appearing outside your door. Many times they come for a word of encouragement or some authentic human contact. It is a different kind of academic mentoring.

"I DON'T KNOW IF IT'S A VISION OR A DILEMMA"—IMPROVING TEACHER EDUCATION

Eventually our conversation moved past Jackie's personal background and early experiences to her perspectives on teacher education. In this part of the conversation she expressed frustration about the way people in the field fail to incorporate a vision of teaching that includes the needs of all children.

Rather than complain about the students who elect to become teachers, Jackie focused on the people whose job it is to prepare them. Despite the concept of academic freedom, we understand that professional preparation must meet certain larger society criteria. For example, doctors must learn standard protocols of diagnosis and treatment. Lawyers must learn appropriate case law to practice in particular jurisdictions. Accountants must learn agreed-upon methods for keeping track of income and expenditures. Increasingly, teacher educators must conform to standards set by state legislatures and state departments of education. Thus teacher educators, at least nominally, should be preparing teachers to work effectively with all students.

Jacqueline Jordan Irvine is clear about her concern that teacher educators take seriously the responsibility to prepare teachers who can work effectively with all students:

> My hope for teacher education is that—and when I say teacher education, I'd better say teacher educators because the students—our students—are simply a reflection of what we've done to them or for them—or not done to them or for them. My hope is that teacher educators will be motivated to implement, design, and evaluate teacher education programs that address the needs of children whom the schools have failed. These are the children who [need help the most], you know. There are children who do well in spite of us, but [so many] children have difficulty in school. And these are not always but sometimes [are] children of color, special needs children, recent immigrant children. But I think the problem is not so much that we don't have teacher education *students* that don't get it. I don't think we have teacher *educators* that get it and don't care [that] they don't get it, and that's sad. My vision—I don't know if it's a vision or a dilemma, depending on what day of the week it is. Sometimes it's just a damn dilemma that I can't solve, and other days it's a vision I'm going to fix.
>
> What's the professional development we need for teacher educators? We think about professional development as a trip to AERA [American Educational Research Association] or AACTE [American Association of Colleges of Teacher Education], and everyone just misses the fact that there is a codified knowledge base on urban and multicultural teacher education that is worth mastering. I think teacher educators think that it's fluff, that it has no theoretical base, and that it's food, fun, and festivals, and that it's something that's not worth my even knowing that there's nothing to know.

As the conversation continued, Jackie drew an analogy between developing new skills for teaching all students and developing new technological skills:

You know what I'm always reminded of? [It's] when I watch my colleagues come up to speed in technology. When the computers first
came out, there were people who decided, "I'm not going to learn
this. I'm going to keep writing on legal yellow pads. But then they
figured out that this [the computer] is important for my work, I must
know this. If I don't know this, I'm going to be left behind." And
people went about various ways [of] getting the skills. Some of them
enrolled in a little course on campus. Other people [were like me]. I
took my computer home and I read my manual and when I needed to
know something, I called my friend Bob. I wasn't going to any course,
I wanted to learn on my own. But we all figured out we couldn't survive in the academy unless we learned this.

I don't want to be left behind, and my White colleagues in technology figured this is important. This makes my work easier. I can't do
without it. Why [can't they develop] the same attitude about multicultural education and urban teacher education? Because they don't think
it makes a difference in their lives.

[Many assume] this too will pass and so the challenge is a challenge of
deans, of colleges of education, department chairs, and teacher educators.

I think there are enough, at least enthusiastic, teacher education
students who want to work in the schools with our children. Now they
may not know what to do when they get there, but at least they have
the first piece . . . "I want to be there." And I think that these kinds
of kids I can work with, these kinds of teacher education students
who are looking to us to help them figure out what to do, and I think
we've failed them miserably and that to me is a vision that we have a
place where teacher educators can come who value what we [African
American teacher educators] know. I think the messenger is as important as the message, [and] as long as the messengers look like me and
you, they don't want to hear the message.

Jackie's last comments speak aloud some of the things that lie beneath the
surface of the teacher education discourse. It does matter who the teacher
educators are, not just to foster "diversity" but also to ensure that a wider
range of perspectives are included in the conversation.

"WHAT DO THE BLACK PEOPLE THINK ABOUT YOU?"—RACIAL
DIFFERENCES IN PROFESSIONAL LIFE

All of the participants in this project were asked to talk about how they
thought their professional lives were different from those of their White colleagues. Perhaps if I were writing from a positivist paradigm, I would have

included a sample of White teacher educators to determine whether or not these perceptions were accurate. However, my work represents a culture-centered approach (King, 1995) that tries to understand social and cultural phenomena from the inside out. If these are the perceptions that people have about their work, their accuracy is not what determines how they function. For example, if White colleagues perceive that Black colleagues are less competent, it does not matter if they are accurate. They treat their Black colleagues as less competent—give them less responsibility, regard their contributions as less significant, and question their actions. Therefore, although perception may be a moving target, it is an important barometer of the social construction of experience and reality.

Throughout our interview, Jackie was clear in relating that she felt fortunate to work at her institution, particularly in her division (or department). "People have been very supportive. I came [here] as an assistant professor with a brand new PhD [and rose] to an endowed chair. I've had many opportunities to move, but Emory has made it worth my while not to move in terms of the support." But she was aware that there were differences in her experiences and those of her White colleagues:

> One way [that our experiences are different] is I spend a great deal of my life where my credibility has been questioned. I don't deal with it. When I say I don't deal [with it], that's off my screen now. I don't deal with this—not that people don't [still] question my credibility. I don't give a damn any more, but unlike my White colleagues, no matter what journal [I] publish in, no matter what awards [I] get and what acknowledgments, it's always still associated with [my] gender and [my] ethnicity. In this instance, "She got it not because she worked hard and read a lot, stayed up all night preparing. It's just that she happened to be in the right place at the right time and it didn't hurt that she was a Black woman."
>
> My White colleagues don't have to deal with that as much. I know some of them are women colleagues who do, but you put the interaction of gender and the race and it really is [tough]. They don't have to deal with racism every day. They don't, you know, walk in elevators and have White ladies draw their pocketbooks close to them. You know they don't worry about their sons and daughters on the street like I worry about my daughter. They don't have to deal with those same issues of racism.

In addition to concerns about racism, Jackie also talked about the reception of her professional success by her parents and others in the Black community. This concern is similar to that expressed by Law (1995), who relates a comment from her working-class mother, "Education destroys something" as a part of "the cruel duality of the working-class student in higher education, some of whom go on to become working-class academics" (p. 1).

> When I got that award at [the Research Focus on Black Education]
> Special Interest Group (SIG) at AERA, I got up and said that my daddy
> would be very proud of me because my daddy would ask me about my
> job when I first started working. He was very concerned, by the way,
> [about] "what the Black people think about what you're doing." And
> when I got that award from the SIG, I said it pleased me a great deal
> because now I can tell my daddy the Black folks thought I was doing all
> right. So, my point of reference is always the Black community. I'm ap-
> preciative of the feedback I get from the White professors, but my person-
> al Black community [that] I've been a part of in Atlanta for 24 years is im-
> portant. I'm accountable to the Black community. It's not extra pressure,
> it's just what is, and so I'm very involved in my church. I have a cadre
> of friends in the community. I feel I must go back in the community, so I
> was a volunteer teacher. I traveled all over with my pastor at the time do-
> ing work in various communities, and I felt that I had to give back. I don't
> know if White professors feel they have to give back to the community. I
> just feel deeply that I have to continue to do that, so there are all kinds of
> levels that my work is different. When a principal calls and says we need
> somebody to come out and do a presentation or something, it doesn't
> help me in the traditional [academic] sense, and in fact, your department
> chair may say, "Don't do all this stuff, it doesn't count for anything," but it
> does count. It counts in the community and I can't say no.

JACQUELINE JORDAN IRVINE'S SCHOLARLY CONTRIBUTION

Although she began her work as a quantitative researcher in the field of educational leadership, Jackie's primary scholarly influence has been in teaching
and teacher education. Her early writings were concerned with issues of
access and African American women in higher education administration.
However, in 1990 she published a book entitled *Black Students and School
Failure: Personnel, Practices, and Prescriptions*. In this book, Jackie refer-
enced the concept of "cultural synchronization," which explores the relationship between macro and micro processes in schooling.

Cultural synchronization involves an understanding of the contexts in
which students live and understand the world—social, economic, and cultural—as well as the contexts of schooling—school organization, classroom
norms, and teacher expectations. Jacqueline Irvine helped us to understand
the complexity of these processes and to better see why so many teachers
were struggling to be effective teachers for students from cultures and backgrounds different from their own.

An important aspect of this work is its application to conceptions of "good" teaching. Jackie began doing this work at a time when national efforts were being directed toward improving teaching. Many of these efforts, though laudable, completely ignored or misunderstood the salience of culture in teaching and learning. Jackie's work began to shine light on the way the surface behaviors of teachers may not be true indicators of their pedagogical skills. For example, she pointed out that a number of seemingly harsh teachers actually were more invested in students' academic success than were many who seemed warm and friendly.

Typical teacher assessments look at one type of teaching as the model for excellence. Teachers who act (and interact) in ways that are consistent with White, middle-class norms often are deemed exemplary. Such teachers may speak to students in a soft, well-modulated voice and make demands on students in the form of personal-need statements or requests. Thus the teacher may say, "I need you to sit down" or "Would you like to have a seat?"

Jackie began documenting the practice of teachers who were more direct and authoritative without being authoritarian. The teachers she observed said things like, "Sit down," without any ambiguity or question as to who was in charge. This more forceful style of communicating with students often was consistent with what they expected of adults. As a consequence the students were more compliant and less class time was taken up with discipline and classroom management.

Although Jackie was careful not to suggest that effective teachers of poor students and students of color were humorless drill sergeants, she worked hard to get the field to recognize that there was more than one way to be effective in the classroom. More important, her work challenged the knowledge producers in the field—scholars of teaching and teacher education—to conceive of teaching excellence more broadly. Instead of celebrating a rather narrow teaching repertoire that made it possible for White, middle-class students to succeed, Jackie's work pointed out that the tradition of excellence that was so long a part of African American culture could be unearthed and showcased to improve teaching and learning for all students.

Indeed, most students who are successful do experience cultural synchronization. Their lives in school closely parallel their lives at home. The way language is used, the opportunities for participation, the reward structures, and the sanctions are amazingly similar. Misbehavior at home warrants a "time-out" and misbehavior at school does also. However, for many working-class and poor students of color, "time-out" is a part of a sporting event. Time-out may seem like a reward. It means having a few moments alone, free from teacher supervision and classwork. Everyone should want a time-out. Unless teachers know what language and techniques have currency in a community, they may regularly be thwarted in their attempts to do simple tasks, such as gain order and have students listen to each other. Jackie's work began to make these differences more transparent in ways that were not stereotypical or prescriptive. Instead, she provided a way to think about teaching as a complex enterprise that challenged both teachers and teacher educators to be more thoughtful about what it means to be a good teacher.

Jackie's work on cultural synchronization represents an important conceptual rubric. But, as is true of the rest of the participants, she also makes a significant contribution to the world of practice. From 1994 until 1998 Jackie directed the Center for Urban Learning/Teaching and Urban Research in Education and Schools (CULTURES). This project was one of two U.S. Department of Education exemplary professional development models for school reform.

The CULTURES program worked with approximately 60 in-service teachers per year to "enhance the success of elementary and middle schools in educating culturally diverse students by providing professional development for teachers" (http://www.emory.edu/IRVINE/CULTURES/, retrieved January 21, 2004). Through a combination of experiences in both the classroom and the community, Jackie was able to build a cadre of teachers committed to teaching all children well. The program melded the best elements of sound professional development in teacher education with emerging research on teaching in culturally diverse schools and communities.

This project worked with small cohorts (15) of teachers with at least 3 years of experience. The teachers participated in cultural immersion experiences in order to see what was available in the community as opposed to relying on taken-for-granted notions that "these children have nothing and come from nothing." Not unlike Luis Moll's (1992) notion of "funds of knowledge," this program focused on students' culture as a source of strength rather than an impediment to learning.

In addition to a cultural immersion experience, the CULTURES program provided teachers with an opportunity to reflect on their practice and improve it. Cohort members got an opportunity to interact with scholars in the field, to observe in classrooms of exemplary teachers, and to develop action research projects to better understand what was happening in their classrooms.

Jackie's vision of true CULTURES program teachers was that they would not only use the experience to improve their own classroom but also become teacher-leaders who helped their colleagues to improve. Just as Harriet Tubman benefited from her ability to escape her oppression and was compelled to keep helping others, Jackie designs her work to create a spirit of liberation in teachers who will not and cannot allow students to languish in classrooms that do not free them intellectually and spur them on academically.

"THE MINUTE WE GET IT, THEY WANT TO CHANGE IT"—MENTORING YOUNG SCHOLARS

Each of the participants in this project had stories to tell about the role of mentoring—either mentoring they received or mentoring they gave. Jackie freely admits that as the first Black faculty member in her department (and among the earliest Black faculty members at Emory University), she realized that she had to cultivate relationships with her White colleagues in order to survive and thrive at the institution:

> What made the difference is that the department chair was a White male [now retired] who made it very clear to everybody in that department that I was valued and really, in an autocratic sense, let them know I was not to be messed with. And people were so afraid of him that they didn't [mess with me].
>
> [Also] Carol [Hahn] had been there 5 years when I got there, and Carol, as a White female, has been my friend for all this time. What made a big difference in my writing and my research is I was not afraid to give my work to Carol and to the department chair. I would get it back. It would be red [penciled], but I knew that they didn't take it and then pass the word around, you know, that Jackie Irvine really doesn't know anything about writing, or Jackie Irvine doesn't know research. What they did was help me by their really, really awesome critique to be a better writer and thinker, I think that's what we all need.

In addition to asking Jackie about the mentoring she received, I asked her about the mentoring she did. She mentioned two junior colleagues by name and went on to describe her process of working with them:

> I'm very convinced [that] tenure is difficult, but tenure is also an initiation ritual. It's learning the rules or rituals, stated to unstated, implicit to explicit. A number of majority males have opportunities [and access to] people [who can] help them understand it, so they try to keep [their sources of information] hidden. So what I try to do is make what's hidden open and, in addition, to provide feedback to, you know, the younger professors. I try to get them to understand what the rules of the game are and, by the way, the minute you try to figure it out, they try to change it. But I think that's my role—to try to help them understand the changing rules of the game. The minute we get it, they want to change it.

"THE LORD DIDN'T PUT YOU HERE FOR NO REASON"—MEANING AND PURPOSE IN AFRICAN AMERICAN SCHOLARS' WORK

As our interview came to a close, Jackie and I had talked over a wide range of topics and, as is often true when conversations transpire between intimates, one ends up exactly where she began. Jackie started off our conversation talking about the role of her parents and her southern upbringing in shaping her future. As we concluded, she talked about the impact of that shaping on her spiritually and how it gave her work a sense of purpose and urgency:

> [To] know where I'm going I have to know where I come from. [The saying that] "The Lord didn't put you here for no reason," that you have a mission, a responsibility, has really shaped my life. I know there are a lot of baaad[1] people out there a lot smarter than me, a whole lot smarter than me, and they're not where I am—and not because I'm so good and so competent. I have been blessed.
>
> [When] people try to get in my way, and I mean in a negative sense—[people] who really try to hurt me—[I] say to them, "You don't know what it was like for me. My parents were not college-educated. I came out of the segregated South. What you're putting in front of me is nothing. I've been there before."
>
> Another African American saying [that defines my work and sense of purpose] is "The Lord didn't bring me this far to leave me." [My] sense of conviction and vision is very much rooted in a spiritual base. You hear words come out of my mouth like *blessing*, about giving back, and that why I think that part of African American culture is real important. In a sense, the African American culture has sustained me.

CONCLUDING THOUGHTS—RESEARCH WITHOUT A SENSE OF PURPOSE TENDS TO LOSE ITS PURPOSE

After sifting through the interview data on Jacqueline Jordan Irvine, I was amazed at the symmetry in our careers and growing-up experiences. Also, I was challenged by her determination to keep her work relevant for her community. Among her final words came a strong statement of the political nature of her work and her commitment to a bigger purpose:

> [There are two expressions that shape my work.] One is a statement made by Peter Cookson that research without a sense of purpose tends to lose its purpose. I like that notion that all research is political and

has purpose. Only when African Americans politicize their work is it critiqued negatively, but all research is political. And research that has no purpose, to me, it's not research, so the idea of advocacy research, which people used to think was an oxymoron when I was being trained, [was not considered] objective.

So I'm into advocacy, learning that has a purpose, and that advocacy is [directed toward] the educational achievement of African American children.

The other I think comes from Pattie Lather, I may be wrong, [but] it's the notion of "What is a university?" She talks about a university as either a museum or a theater. I like those metaphors, and she says it's the powers that be—and this is my spin on that—White people welcome us into the university as a museum. They want us to look at it and [not] touch anything—stand back and admire, and go, "Ooooh, isn't that pretty?" And don't try to put *your* piece on the wall.

Jackie continues with the metaphor and explains what she believes is the role of African American scholars in opting for the other vision of the academy:

There's a notion of a university as street theater, where it's always in [the] process of being created and re-created, and I like that idea—where everyone has a part. Sometimes you're acting in a role, sometimes you're writing a script, sometimes you're producing and directing.

I think the entry of African Americans into the academy [means] we've changed it to a theater—a free theater, and they want to keep it a museum.

Jackie's desire to change the institution also reminds me of Harriet Tubman. Tubman was not only unwilling to settle for a slave existence for herself, she was also unwilling to settle for a slave existence for any human being. Similarly, Jackie Irvine has directed her career toward a higher purpose and insisted that the students with whom she works move in that same direction. I imagine her metaphorically urging her scholars with the words, "Dead folks tell no tales."

NOTE

1. The term *bad* is an African American colloquialism that means just the opposite. Jackie is referring to the many very good scholars and thinkers she knows.

SIX

Geneva Gay

Biddy Mason

Although I studied United States history in undergraduate school and taught it for almost 10 years in the Philadelphia Public School system,[1] it was not until I moved to California in the 1970s that I learned about a woman named Biddy Mason. Her story is an important one in the African American struggle for freedom and equality.

Biddy Mason was born August 15, 1818, in Mississippi. She was enslaved on a plantation owned by Robert and Rebecca Smith. As she grew to young adulthood, Biddy became a mother to three daughters, Ellen, Ann, and Harriet. The latter child's father was thought to be Robert Smith himself. In 1847 Robert Smith converted to Mormonism and moved his household, including the slaves, to the Utah territory. This was a 2,000-mile trek across rugged country, and Biddy Mason was responsible for herding the cattle, preparing the meals, acting as midwife, and providing childcare.

In 1851 Robert Smith again moved his household, this time to San Bernardino, California, to be a part of a Mormon community that Brigham Young was starting there. Smith either did not know or did not give any thought to the fact that California had come into the Union in 1850 as a free state where slavery was outlawed. However, Biddy Mason knew what it meant to be in California, and through a series of legal maneuvers she became a part of a petition to the court and in 1856 won freedom for herself and her children. She later moved to Los Angeles where she worked as a nurse and a midwife. Her hard work allowed her to become financially independent.

What is interesting about Mason's story is that she was a contemporary of Dred Scott, who also filed suit to gain his freedom after his slave owner had taken him to live for extended periods of time in Illinois and Wisconsin, two free states. Scott fought from 1847 to 1857 but was denied his freedom at the Supreme Court level. Much of our historical focus has been on Dred Scott, but Biddy Mason proved the year before the Dred Scott decision that such a legal strategy was possible.

Mason's intelligence and business acumen were evident when just 10 years after she won her freedom she purchased property in Los Angeles for $250. Allegedly, she instructed her daughters never to abandon this property. Mason was one of the first Black women to own property in Los Angeles. Mason's property is located in what became the center of the Los Angeles commercial district. In 1884 she sold a parcel of her land for $1,500 and on the remaining land built a commercial building with rental spaces. Mason continued making smart business and real estate decisions and eventually she accumulated a fortune of almost $300,000, which had about the buying power of $5.5 million in 2003.

In addition to becoming wealthy, Mason was also a very generous woman. She gave to many charities that provided food and shelter for the poor, regardless of race. It was not unusual to see lines of needy people forming outside her Spring Street home. In 1872 she and her son-in-law, Charles Owens, founded and financed Los Angeles's first Black church, a branch of the First African Methodist Episcopal church.

Biddy Mason died on January 15, 1891, and was buried at Evergreen Cemetery in Los Angeles. Almost 100 years later, a tombstone was erected on her unmarked gravesite at a ceremony attended by almost 3,000 members of the First African Methodist Episcopal Church. Today, First African Methodist Episcopal Church is one of the most impressive congregations in the United States serving about 18,000 members.

"STUMBLING BACKWARDS IN BLIND FAITH"—GENEVA GAY'S EARLY STORY

Geneva Gay (like Carl Grant and James Banks) is a legendary figure in the minds of most African American scholars in education. We recognize people like Geneva as pioneers who took the risks and suffered the repercussions for challenging the dominant paradigm. I first remember seeing her image in a journal article. At the end of the article there was a little thumbnail photo of her. In that photo her hair was a lovely crown of natural hair, à la Angela Davis. I recall catching my breath and thinking, "This must be one tough sister." I realized that the academy worked hard to get Blacks to conform to dominant norms and representations. In that photo

Geneva Gay seemed to be saying, "This is me. Deal with it!"

My first face-to-face meeting with Geneva took place almost 15 years ago. Once again I was struck by her countenance. She seemed so elegant and self-possessed. When I think of her, I am reminded of Jackie Irvine's comments about the "good-looking Black women with briefcases." Geneva could easily be mistaken for a fashion model—not just because she is tall, slender, attractive, and stylish. She is a real presence. You always know when she is in the room. However, like each of the participants in this project, she has a compelling story about her beginnings.

Hers is a story of very humble beginnings that seem almost incompatible with her distinguished professor persona with which most of the academic world is familiar:

> I grew up in rural Georgia in a very extremely poor and very uneducated family, unfortunately. I grew up with my grandmother who probably had only about 3 years of formal education. So in some ways getting to an academic life just defies all kinds of even miraculous odds, if you will. The only thing that I can figure out that might be an indirect linkage to being in the academic community is I was always interested in reading and stuff like that.
>
> [I grew] up in a rural community, and I mean a really [hard] working [community], because we were tenant farmers and [had] to work our own land and we worked this land with basic human labor, you know, with a minimum amount of mechanical assistance. And as a little child I always kept saying, in my head, "There has to be an easier way to make a living." That was the only thing I could think of.

As she entered adolescence, Geneva saw herself as somewhat different from her family and local peers. High school provided a window to a wider world and she was willing to explore that world:

> I didn't really have any belief that I could find a way out of [rural poverty], but I was willing to put myself in the way of some different options and when I went to high school my network of friends happened to be academic types. They were performing well in school, everybody was talking about going to college and all that, so I was in that set because I performed well academically, so in that sense I [was] already kind of marginal from my home community. [I was also] a bit marginal [at school] because for the most part they were city kids and I was a rural child, so I was kind of on the edge, but at least it was a point of identity so that if they were talking about going to college, then I talked about going to college even though inside I never believed it was possible.
>
> I was able to go to college because [when] I finished high school,

I went back to live with my mother again who had years before migrated to Ohio. [Since] she was in Ohio I could go to a local college—almost free. That's the way I decided [to go to college]. It was kind of like stumbling backwards in blind faith that something like this could happen.

Geneva entered undergraduate school at the University of Akron in Ohio and, like most of the project participants, points to an African American teacher who inspired her:

All I remember is [a] social studies teacher, and her name was Fannie Pugh and one reason why she comes to mind is because of the way in which she engaged with students. She was a young teacher, she seemed to have a sense of being able to connect with young people. She had a sort of playful way of teaching but at the same time was entirely demanding of one's performance, so I think about Fannie a lot. Here was this woman demonstrating that you could have high academic standards, insist the kids perform, and at the same time find ways to bring about that communal [feeling] where the teacher is bonding with kids as humans.

However, what is different about Geneva's perspective about her inspiration is the way she considered what one might term an "inspiration from the bottom," where the students with whom she worked served as the impetus for her growth:

I taught in Akron, Ohio, at a central city school that was overwhelmingly Black. I can recall [my] trying to be an institutional person [where] students would do things [and] would give me reality feedback. So they would bring up the subjects [and say], "You don't believe that," so I think my students recognized contradictions in me long before I did. Part of the reason [I went] to graduate school was to find out what I was and what I was about. I still think that my students, by pointing to contradictions in me, were probably the first ones to locate some directions for me even before I was aware that they were going to come, and I still say that I went into multicultural education because of those kids.

"GOING TO BE AS BLACK AS I WANT TO BE"—GRADUATE SCHOOL AS AN IDENTITY WATERSHED

Geneva described her graduate school experience as one where she would truly come to know herself and determine the kind of professional she would be. In general, her graduate school experience was positive, and she credits that to her adviser, O. L. Davis of the University of Texas at Austin. Unlike Joyce King and Carl Grant whose journeys to graduate school seemed more serendipitous or Jackie Irvine who had purposed in her mind from her early childhood to become a college professor, Geneva Gay went to graduate school on a personal and specific mission:

> I went to graduate school for a master's degree at Akron University, but my PhD degree was at the University of Texas at Austin. And, as it turns out, at the time when I went to graduate school, I really was going more in search of myself, you know, like, "Who is Geneva?" Is this "Miss Gay" that I was trying to be [in] the schools or is it "Geneva"? And I can recall having conversations with myself [about], "Which one are you going to be? First of all, are there two of you? And which one are you going to be? Are you going to be Miss Gay that was kind of artificial or are you going to be Geneva?"
>
> The other thing was I still had not—at the point of going to graduate school—figured out with myself [how to be] at peace with me as an African American. I mean, I was doing things like, you know, engaging in self-deprivation, being intimidated and threatened to the point of almost inaction by other people. So that was another way I was going in search of myself and saying, "How are you going to do this thing called life? Are you going to be apologetic for being an African American, or what?" So I went to graduate school to find myself and I recall [what I said] to the person that became my major professor, O. L. Davis, when he called me and said [I] had been admitted. [He asked] "Are you coming?" and I said to him over the phone after finally [saying] "Yeah, I'll come," I said "I'm coming to Texas, going to be as Black as I want to be. Can you all handle it?' And O. L.'s response was something to the effect of, "Yeah, we can. We can deal with that."
>
> As a result (of O. L. Davis's encouragement), the greatest thing for me for my graduate training was I found myself, you know, I found a way to be African American, to hook into my culture, to find my sense of ethics and integrity that would serve me, I think—serve me well by my own standards both professionally and personally, thereafter. And for part of that I thank O. L. for being aggressive and recruiting students of color. [He] possibly saw some potential in me [in] that he came after me. I didn't go after him, and then when I was there he was open enough to let me think aloud with him about what was important to me. He provided me those opportunities, so that was good.
>
> [Later on] another kind of scholarly mentor [for me] was (and is) Jim Banks. Over time, Jim has been a really good mentor for me.

Earlier he provided quite a few opportunities to write, and not only to write, but you know very well when you write for Jim you meet deadlines. I'm not a very disciplined writer, but I honored his demand and respect his scholarship and his professional place, and when I've agreed to accept invitations from him, I've delivered on time.

GENEVA GAY'S SCHOLARLY CONTRIBUTION

As a student of curriculum and teacher education at Stanford I had the opportunity to study carefully the history and theories of U.S. curriculum. Names such as Kliebard, Dewey, Apple, Tyler, and Schwab became familiar parts of my daily conversations. Often I wondered if there were any African Americans who contributed to our curriculum history. Fortunately, a long talk with Stanford scholar Sylvia Wynter helped me see that Carter G. Woodson, in his classic, *The Mis-Education of the Negro* (1933/1990), had spoken to curriculum issues more than a half century ago.

Later, I would find another African American curriculum theorist who plunged into the field of multicultural education with the rigor and discipline of curriculum theory. That scholar is Geneva Gay. Her chapter "Curriculum Theory and Multicultural Education" in the *Handbook of Research on Multicultural Education* (Banks & Banks, 2004) is the most authoritative voice on the subject. Geneva also is known for her work on ethnic identity development. In her article "Implications of Selected Models of Ethnic Identity Development for Educators" (1985), Geneva explores how educators might benefit from understanding the developmental nature of ethnic identity. Knowing, for example, that students continue to grapple with questions of who they are provides teachers with more information concerning what materials to select, what pedagogical styles may meet with more success, and what management and discipline strategies are most useful.

Another important aspect of Geneva's work is made evident in a book, *Expressively Black* (1987), that she edited with Willie Baber. In this book, Geneva reveals the cultural connections that are present throughout the Black world. She and her coeditor look at Black style, kinship relations, family ties, communication styles, leadership, music, religion, art, and theater as cultural artifacts of the distinctive culture of Black folks. For example, in one chapter there is a discussion of city ways and country ways. Rather than focus on geopolitical or citizenship loyalties as a social binder, they look at the way the culture prevails transnationally. Thus they identify a cultural connection between rural Africans and rural African Americans in speech styles, hospitality protocols, and other forms of interaction.

In my opinion, *Expressively Black* (1987) is one of the more under-rated aspects of Geneva Gay's work. I think it represents a bold move away from the provincial nature of much of the early work in ethnic studies and multicultural education to include a more international picture of culture and ethnicity. Given our growing awareness of globalization and cross-cultural and international changes, I believe it is exactly the kind of work that deserves a second look.

Finally, I would call attention to Geneva Gay's (2000) work in culturally responsive teaching. In this book, Geneva raises a fundamental question about the paradox of students of color who find success in many aspects of their lives yet struggle to be successful in the classroom. She undergirds her argument with a series of assertions about students' strengths (e.g., culture, diversity) versus institutional limitations (e.g., conventional reform, intention without action, narrow forms of assessment). By using several case examples of success in communities of color, Geneva offers what I term "existence proofs" for what is possible when teachers practice culturally responsive teaching. Of course, because my own research agenda converges so nicely with this aspect of Geneva's work, I cannot pretend to be the least bit objective about her work. I do believe that teacher educators must take pedagogy seriously. In fact, over time I have become intellectually more seduced by pedagogy than by curriculum. It is not just what we teach students, but also how we teach them that is key to their success in the classroom. Geneva Gay has known this for many years and it remains a hallmark of her career.

"MY PERSONAL IS THE HEART AND SOUL OF MY PROFESSIONAL"— GENEVA GAY AS TEACHER EDUCATOR

As we began to explore the places where Geneva's professional identity came to fruition, the conversation regularly moved back to her growing up and growing sense of self. Like most of the participants, she lives and breathes in a world that her intimates—parents, family members, childhood friends—know little about. However, her experiences with these people have profoundly shaped the professional she was to become:

> My professional activities always begin, center, [and] end in [an] autobiographical point of reference because what drives me to do what I do is [my] memory of me. It's kind of like the notion of the child within, and I think that child within has grown to healthiness but I remember when that child was not healthy. I want to say to myself that not only did Geneva exist; I think that there are many approximations

of Geneva—that there are many, many African American kids first, and my point of reference starts with African Americans and then I extend beyond [that]. That's another element of what I say is autobiographical. My personal is the heart and soul of my professional. It's the bottom line, center of why I do the kinds of things I do, and I have no qualms with saying that if I take a position, a professional position, or an idea that I'm trying to argue—if I can't make them meaningful to some personal life experiences, if not my own, [or those of] somebody I know, or somebody I imagine, then it's not worth spending time and energy on. [I say this] because I carry in my head, when I'm trying to argue a point, somebody, I mean a real person, [who] is symptomatic of many people that I'm concerned about. As I write, as I present, I'm speaking about, for, and to that person. I don't separate the professional and the personal.

I also made a commitment to myself that wherever I go and whatever I do, in all that I would do, I would try to make sure that my multiple meanings hold forth. So in the classroom I refuse to just be a professor. There are all kinds of ways [that] I just make sure that my multiple meanings become critical.

Like several of the other participants, Geneva has a family that is less cognizant of her work and its meaning. They know that she is a professor but have limited understanding of what that entails. They probably know less about the impact of her work and how it has touched countless students, teachers, and scholars throughout the world:

Here's the thing. My mothers doesn't have . . . I mean she knows that I teach [at] someplace called a college, but that's about as much as she [understands] because she has no point of reference of what college is about. So one of the things that I do is to try not to even inadvertently entice my family to play that . . . you know, put me on a pedestal and all that kind of stuff. So what I have done along the way is make sure that I know how to engage with my family, and I'm very serious about that and very deliberate about it because I think my education should teach me those skills. If I'm educated, I should be able to maneuver in many different settings, not require my uneducated mother or grandmother (when she was alive) to accommodate me. So over the years I have learned ways to accommodate the people in my family that are just eons away from me existentially and how I live my life.

Although Geneva talks about the distance between her world and that of her family, I am aware that she does reach out to include her family in aspects of her world. For many years her nephews/godchildren spent summer vacations with her where she introduced them to the world that is made possible by education. She did not lecture the boys but rather helped them see that there was some advantage to persisting in education. The payoff could be in the form of a more comfortable personal life. Of course, Geneva is also clear that with such privilege comes great responsibility.

At the same time she reaches out, she carefully guards her private time with her family. She is appreciative of her family's support of her scholarly efforts, but she does not want to her work to be the basis for her relationship with her family:

> When I go home, you know, I don't let Dr. Gay get in the way. You know, I learned that in graduate school. I learned that I had to leave Geneva Gay, PhD, out of my personal and familial interactions and I still do that to this day. So I change my language. I change my points of reference. I change the topics of interest that I'm discussing when I'm interacting with my family, because if I talked with them about issues that I might be talking [about] with you, it just gets in the way. Now that doesn't mean that some of the issues are not the same, but how we engage with them is very, very different.

GETTING "DOWN AND DIRTY" TO TEACH—THE PEDAGOGY OF GENEVA GAY

Although Geneva talks about using a new lexicon and repertoire in her interactions with her family, she clearly brings some of what she learned from her background and family experiences into her life in the academy. Her respect for teaching and the work of the pedagogue is powerful. She stands out among the project participants as someone whose passion for teaching occupies a major portion of her scholarly life:

> I'm an unorthodox teacher, let's say professor, so I work very diligently at not [presenting an] image as a traditional professor, and as it turns out, it works well for me. My approach to pedagogy is quite different. One of the things that I do [is] confrontational teaching. I'm willing to do almost anything, you know. I would get down and dirty, and again I'm speaking metaphorically, almost through cultural [lenses], but I get down and dirty to teach. You know, I'm a teacher before scholar. I'm a teacher-scholar rather than a scholar-teacher so I work hard at teaching and I think you have an obligation—a real ethical [responsibility]— a competence obligation when you stand in front of a group

in the role of teacher to do something other than just go and spew out information.

I take my role as teacher very seriously, to engage, to challenge, to probe, all those kinds of things that we would imagine [would] go into good pedagogy. I'm trying to live that and I'm trying to find ways to get everybody in those classes somehow or another engaged during some portion of the time when they're with me. I use a very mobile approach to my pedagogy. I'm kind of all over the place, if you will, so I think that what I may have done with students is to demonstrate that you can be in the academy and you don't have to be bored. That there's a way of being in [the] university and there is a craft, a talent to teaching that can be demonstrated here.

I think my teaching provides a very, very different look at what being a student and a teacher is and what a university is like because I think there's some very, very horrible notions about what teaching is in a university.

Geneva's perspectives on teaching in the university also give some insights into her perspectives on what it is like to be a part of mainstream institutional culture. Her comments about the institutions themselves and the differences between her work and that of her colleagues are instructive:

After I left public school teaching, I've always taught in large state institutions—I mean very large and always White. This is my third university I've taught in. I taught at the University of Texas, Purdue University, and University of Washington, and they're all—to say predominantly White is to be overly generous. They are extremely predominantly White. And that's . . . fine. I've made that a deliberate choice to stay in those if for no other reason than I like the anonymity of the crowd. And then, beyond that, as time goes on, I think that what has become a reason why I've stayed in those kinds of institutions is because these are the people that are going to teach our children, and I want to [use] my professional energy trying to work with people that are going to be the ones that will impact our children.

"YOU'VE GOT TO BE IN ROLE"—DIFFERENCES IN BLACK AND WHITE ACADEMIC LIFE

One of the challenges that all the project participants addressed was the degree to which they perceived their professional lives to be different from those of their White colleagues. All of the participants were able to identify differences but none regarded the differences as so burdensome that they impeded their career trajectories. Indeed, this project is comprised of scholars who are exceptionally successful. They have name recognition and stature in the field. The sense I got from the participants was that working harder and doing more come with the territory. This theme was apparent in Geneva's comments:

> Well, first of all, I think my White colleagues don't work nearly as hard as I do. I think another thing is that my White colleagues probably have much more relaxation about what they do, in the sense that some people talk about it as [their having] that notion of taken-for-grantedness.
>
> I am always conscious of [factors] that I don't think my White colleagues even enter into their realm of reality or even have to concern themselves about. Like, for example, I think that in my professional life I always have to be ready to grapple with some variation of racism, whereas my White colleagues don't even have to wonder about whether racism will exist. [It] requires me [to] spend a certain kind of energy, attending energy, just being at attention all the time. So you might say, sort of metaphorically speaking, [that in] my life in the academy, especially the environments I've chosen to work in, I'm always on stage. [It's as if] I'm always on stage, as if—let's say we are in a theater where my White colleagues [are] the audience. If you're an actor on the stage, you don't have the luxury of relaxing. You've got to be in role. You've got to be in character all the time, whereas if you're in the audience, you just came to relax, to recreate. So in some ways it's almost like I think maybe my White colleagues can approach their work with a sense of relaxation that I, as a person of color, can't. Now that doesn't mean that I wake up every morning and say "Woe [is] me," but I do think there is a [higher] level of dealing, of attending to tasks, because of [our] being so visible, of being so exposed all the time. Personally, I've found ways to deal with that, but I think with younger scholars of color it can be extremely draining. It can be a source of stress and anxiety.
>
> I'm increasingly concerned about [that]. When I've got graduate students reaching the conclusion of their programs and going into their careers, I'm more and more trying to have conversations around how you stay healthy in the academy. And [by] staying healthy, I mean healthy as a person so that you're not just producing academically and you end up losing yourself or your sense of integrity, or possibly sacrificing your personal relationships.

Despite the challenge African American teacher education scholars face in the academy, Geneva is not pessimistic about her work. Instead, she chooses to focus on the rewards of teaching and is exuberant about her teaching:

> The thing I think I demonstrate is that teaching and learning can be a joyous venture, that you can have joy en route. Another thing I think I demonstrate is that truly teaching and learning are partnerships, so my students and I work together at the business of learning. So, when I learn something from them, we celebrate it together. When they learn from me, we celebrate together and I think—for my White students, my majority students— I think I demonstrate to them that there is joy in diversity and you don't need to be fearful about it. [It's] like—there is something lovely to be had here, come on join us—and [I] kind of help them get in touch with their own diversity. For my students of color, probably the most powerful thing for them is that [realization] that you can be in this place and you don't have to sell your soul. You know that you can be an academic, very serious, very successful, and still be culturally connected, ethnically affiliated. I'm very serious about that.

Geneva's optimism about her teaching does not translate into a similar upbeat view of her impact on the institutions in which she has worked. She's realistic about the limits of individuals on institutions that are entrenched in norms and patterns of operating that exclude alternate perspectives. When asked what impact she thought she had on her department and institution, Geneva responded:

> Not very much, unfortunately, and that's a sad thing to say some 25 years later—you know, 20 plus years later. But the sad part about it is I think as long as I am there, physically present, [I could have an] impact, if for no other reason than [the] so-called canonical notions about what [constitutes] a successful academic. I mean I've got those. I've got the scholarship; I've got the tenure; I've got the rank and all that. So when I'm there, you cannot not attend to me, you know, because of that. If nothing else, people will honor those things, but unfortunately, if I'm not on the attack then my issues that I'm trying to promote and trying to advocate for will get set aside. And it happens all the time. I think the unfortunate thing is that my issues have not been institutionalized. If they were, then I wouldn't have to be present and on the case, and having to remind people that you have over[looked] this, yet again. [It's] knowing that if I'm present and keep my mouth shut, more than likely the diversity issue would not be attended to, you know, [that] it still has to come from me.

It's kind of humbling—and frustrating to know that after all this time that when I step away from this [and] retire, there may not be much left.

"AFFIRMATION BEFORE REFORMATION"—THE ESSENCE OF GENEVA GAY

I began this chapter with a discussion of Biddy Mason and argue that she is symbolic of the grit and integrity of Geneva Gay. Biddy understood the rules of the game and was adept at deploying them to secure her freedom. She knew that the nation was not conceived with her best interests at heart. Similarly, Geneva understands that the academy does not always function in her best interest as an African American woman. Despite its failure to do so, Geneva has found ways to make her mark in the academy while simultaneously calling it to task for its shortcomings. Throughout our discussion, she reiterated her commitment to maintaining a true and genuine self:

[The most important thing] for me personally is be real, be for real. There are a few things that get my hackles up, but I don't let other people's mess do too much with it—but one thing I can't stand is hypocrisy and superficiality. So whatever I'm trying to do, I try to be genuine. Now other people may have issues with that, but I don't care, I'm genuine by my standards, so I've got a set of criteria inside of me that I say whatever I'm going to do, I've got to live up to this sort of ethical code of mine, and part of that is that you don't engage in hypocrisy and you try to be as authentic as you possibly can.

On a more professional level, I guess if I were going to pull one [a slogan or proverb] out, you know we can't do that with just one, but it's probably "affirmation before reformation." I find myself using that a lot and trying to sort of give a direction or give a sense of an ideological point to anchor oneself, or one's agenda. What I've been doing with that is saying to my students, to other people, [that] we ought to assign ourselves as advocates before we ask anybody to reform. I think that is pedagogical power, that's political power. You know implicit within that is . . . whatever it is, you've got to find something worthy of affirmation, so you sometimes have to really dig deep to find it.

Part of Geneva's affirmation is found in her identification with African American culture. Despite her desire to maintain some level of anonymity within the institutional setting and her acknowledgment of the social distance that exists between her and her family, Geneva declares a strong affiliation with African American culture:

The notion of struggle is [a big part of] African American culture. We know that struggle is our reality and we have found a way to honor struggle, even embraced some [notion] of aesthetics of struggle. My thing is that what that does for me is to expect to struggle. If I'm not struggling, I probably would wonder "What's going on here?" You know, something is not quite right here. Another [aspect of African American culture] is the incredible ability to bounce back. Some people, and I probably won't capture [it] the way we say it in our own culture, but it's the [idea] to make a way out of no way. In some ways I get greater joy out of taking nothing or virtually nothing and turning it into something imaginative and creative, and I think the other thing that's done for me is it's been kind of an intellectual practice so that I'm almost never, ever content [just] to reach deeper. I want to look for other possibilities in all of this and now I'm finding that I see that in my own writing, my own talking.

Geneva continues her notion of affirmation in her work in curriculum and teacher education and in her work with young scholars:

My vision [for teacher education] would be [that] at the level of curriculum, I would like to see a strong multicultural presence permeated throughout everything that teachers are exposed to, from admission through certification, and recertification. At the personnel [level] of teacher education, my vision is that no one would ever be hired without some minimum competency in diversity. The other thing that I would like to see [is] that multicultural education permeated throughout.

What I'd like to see is people in teacher education stop placing the burden of multicultural education on getting more people of color into teacher ed. That's not going to happen in the next 20 years, so the reality is we will have White females doing this [teaching in our schools], so let's get busy and make sure that they are adequately prepared to work with children of color.

About affirming young scholars, Geneva says the following:

Probably three fourths of my graduate students end up being personal friends, and I've stayed in touch with them beyond graduate studies as colleagues, and of [those] two thirds [constitute] a smaller core where we're still in touch and we do mentoring kinds of things.

Of the [former students] I have in mind there are at least five who are African American and they are at different institutions now and we are still in touch periodically. Most of them now have just gotten promotion to associate professor. So we still talk about things and living in the community—the academic community—publishing opportunities. [I say to them,] "Here's an idea that you might want to consider. As I listen to you talk, have you thought about writing this?" Or things like, "Well, you're doing this, maybe you ought not to be spending your time working at that professional conference but why not consider this one? You'll get greater mileage out of those kinds of things."

As I reread the transcript of my interview with Geneva, I was quickly brought back to the life of Biddy Mason. Demaratus (2002) reports that after Judge Benjamin Hayes ruled that Biddy had a right to her freedom as a resident of California, she became a midwife and a nurse during the cholera and smallpox epidemics. Figuratively, Geneva is a midwife of multicultural education curriculum as well as many up-and-coming scholars of education. Giving birth to anything is difficult. That is why the birthing process is called labor. Geneva's closing words capture her role of midwife, coach, and colaborer in the work of improving teaching and teacher education: "The disposition to struggle has become a part of [my] intellectual persona."

NOTE

1. Resources for this section include J. C. Smith, Ed., *Epic Lives: One Hundred Black Women Who Made a Difference,* Canton, MI: Visible Ink Press, 1993; T. Bolden, *The Book of African American Women: 150 Crusaders, Creators, and Uplifters,* Avon, MA: Adams Media Corporation, 1996; and D. Demaratus, *The Force of a Feather: The Search for a Lost Story of Slavery and Freedom,* Salt Lake City: University of Utah Press, 2002.

SEVEN

William Tate

Nat Turner

On the morning of August 22, 1831, eight Black slaves, led by a preacher named Nat Turner, entered a home in Southampton County, Virginia, owned by the Travis family.[1] Turner and his followers killed five members of the Travis family. This incident marked the beginning of an uprising of enslaved Africans that lasted for 36 hours. By the time the insurrection was quelled, some 60 or 70 slaves had joined with Turner to kill 58 White people in and around an area east of Richmond.

Nat Turner was born into slavery in Virginia in 1800 and as a child he was overheard describing events that preceded his birth. This was thought by some other Blacks to indicate that Nat was a prophet. Nat himself believed that he was chosen by God to be a preacher and became a deeply religious man. He claimed to have had several visions that directed many of his actions.

In 1821 Turner ran away from his overseer but returned after about a month because of a vision in which he was told to return to his earthly master. After the death of his slave master, Samuel Turner, Nat was sold to Thomas Moore. Several years later Turner had another vision in which he saw drops of blood on field corn. On May 12, 1828, Turner had a third vision that he believed was a call to arms to rise up and kill his enemies when he was given an appropriate sign.

In 1830 Turner was moved to the home of Joseph Travis, the new husband of his previous owner's widow. Turner described Travis as a kind master, but in February 1831 when there was a solar eclipse, Turner believed he received his sign. Turner plotted with four other enslaved Africans to begin a rebellion. Although the group originally planned to start the uprising on July 4, 1831, Turner's unexpected illness forced them to abort the plan.

On August 13, 1831, an atmospheric disturbance caused the sun to take on a bluish-green color. Turner took this as the final sign and a week later, on August 21, he and six men set their plan in motion. At 2 a.m. the men entered the Travis household and killed the entire sleeping family. Over the next day and a half, Turner and his men marched toward Jerusalem, Virginia, where they were met by a group of White militia. After that encounter Turner and his men scattered, attempted to attack another house, but were repelled. Several of Turner's men were captured, and the remaining rebels were subdued when they met up with state and federal troops in a final confrontation. At this clash, one slave was killed and many escaped, including Nat Turner. In the end, Nat Turner and his men had killed between 55 and 60 people.

From the time of this last skirmish until October 30, 1831, Turner hid out in several places throughout Southampton County where he was captured. Turner's "confession" to Thomas R. Gray, a physician, was taken while he was in the county jail. Much of what we know about Turner comes from this document that was as much a treatise about his life and purpose as a confession of guilt. Turner was tried in the Southampton County Court on November 5 and sentenced to death by hanging. He was hanged, and then skinned, on November 11.

The state of Virginia executed 55 people associated with this insurrection. It also reimbursed slaveholders for their slaves, but this incident fueled a climate of hysteria that led to the death by White mobs of about 200 Black people, most of whom had nothing to do with Turner's rebellion.

"JUST SHOW UP ON THE FIRST DAY"—THE EARLY LIFE OF WILLIAM TATE

Anyone who knows Bill Tate might be shocked to see him compared to Nat Turner. Bill is kind, rational, and level-headed. However, those who know him well know that a special fire burns beneath that cool exterior. As his friend and colleague, I have been privy to that side of his personality and have seen it at work in his scholarship, teaching, and service. Some might suggest that a better comparison for Bill would be Booker T. Washington because of the congruence of both men's perspective on self-help.

But Bill has neither Washington's skill at deceit nor his desire to be acknowledged by the mainstream. Rather, like Turner, Bill has a fire for justice and a gift for rhetoric and leadership. Historian Eric Foner (1971) identifies Turner as a man of great intellect and leadership capabilities. "Turner's role as the organizer of a slave rebellion cannot be understood unless his position of leadership among the slaves of Southampton is remembered; it was a leadership voluntarily accorded to him by the slaves themselves" (p. 2).

From his early days, Bill Tate was a leader. Bill grew up in Chicago, Illinois, the eldest of three boys, and attended Holy Angels Catholic School. His experiences at Holy Angels were pivotal in defining who he would be. This catholic school on Chicago's South side is most recognized for its outspoken and culturally centered priest, Father Gene Clemons. Clemons became widely known for his "one child, one church" program that advocated each Black catholic parish to adopt at least one African American child out of foster care. To prove his dedication to this project, Clemons decided to adopt a child himself, in the face of opposition from the bishop, the cardinal, and the Vatican itself.

Bill left Holy Angels to attend high school at Chicago's Archbishop Quigley Preparatory Seminary. He was a good student who everyone believed would attend college. Bill himself was less certain, wondering how he would finance a college education:

> I realized after high school I didn't have the revenue to go to college, but the tradition I came out of just said, "Boy, just show up on the first day." The first day I showed up at Northern [Illinois University] I didn't have a dorm room and I didn't have a dime, but the tradition I came out of said you can get it together on your own, pull yourself up by your bootstraps. I was able to negotiate with the university to give me a room on the pre-law floor because that was the only room not filled up at the time. [I] met with some people in financial aid and filled out some forms to be an independent student and they just—by the Grace of Almighty God—said, "I can't believe you showed up here without any of this." That was enough. The people just basically stood by me right through the first semester, got [me] financial aid, and the rest is history. But I think it comes from this tradition of . . . a lot of kids today, [I think] they just give up and if you don't have a series of successes in your own context, you will give up. The context I came out of was we were dirt poor, the school [Holy Angels] was dirt poor, but somehow doors kept opening up. Somehow the electricity bills just got paid. Somehow it just happened and when you have that kind of experience, I think it gives you a whole other outlook on life in general. These jobs at these very, very elitist institutions, in particular— you're not intimidated. I mean, it's just another group of people—you have to figure out what the system is and move on. So I think I came out of [a] very, very strong, pride-filled [background], and I don't mean

pride in a negative way. I mean proud of being intellectuals, of standing up for something to make a contribution to society and to people.

After negotiating his way through Northern Illinois University, Bill became a teacher in the Dallas, Texas, Public School system and almost immediately began to think about graduate school. Although he did not have a clear vision of what he wanted to study and how he wanted to shape his career, he knew there was more out there for him to do:

> I started my career as a secondary mathematics teacher in the Dallas Public Schools and I was interested in going to grad school as a teacher, get[ting] a math degree at the master's level. At that point I basically ran into . . . I was fortunate enough to have a couple [of] people in my life who encouraged me to go forward. One was a professor who taught cognitive science, a math course. He happened to be African American and one of the few Black faculty members at the University of Texas at Dallas, and he indicated that there was this career called math education which I really had never thought about. I was thinking about just doing math or going back to economics. [I also got] encouragement from my father and his good friend who got a PhD in education from Ohio State. The three of them were very encouraging about going back.
>
> At that time I had a good relationship with a woman, Roz Einstein, who was a professor at Texas Women's University. She suggested that I get out of Texas, and she was a graduate of the University of Maryland and [she] thought it would be a better fit for what I was trying to do, and that's what I did. I followed her lead and talked to her major professor, Martin Johnson, who again was an African American in mathematics education. He welcomed me with open arms to Maryland and I completed my degree.

TAKING BABY PICTURES—MY RELATIONSHIP WITH BILL TATE

One of the basic premises of this project is that I would select only participants whom I know well because the intimacy would allow me to ask more penetrating and personal questions. However, selecting friends and associates made my role as portraitist one of an interested party rather than a neutral observer. I am working to present the participants in their best light.

Bill Tate is the only participant who is not a senior scholar (in relation to me) or an age-cohort peer. Bill is my "little brother" in the academy and as such, I found myself handling the data from his interview like a mother hen. I want his "picture" to look good. I am metaphorically slicking back his hair and adjusting his tie. But, like most mothers at the portrait studio, I already have a great looking baby. My fussing is more about me than about him. There really was little I could do to enhance the portrait because what he presents is exactly the picture I have always seen.

Bill and I came to the University of Wisconsin-Madison together in the fall of 1991. I was recruited from Santa Clara University and came to Wisconsin having used about 2 years on my tenure clock. Bill was a newly-minted PhD from the University of Maryland. As a part of his start-up, the department offered Bill the Anna Julia Cooper postdoctoral fellowship. This provided Bill with a year to get his research started without the responsibility of teaching and committee service.

With our offices on the same floor we spent many hours visiting and sharing with each other. I remember going into Bill's office one day not long after having arrived at Wisconsin and asking him, "Now just what is it that you study?" He responded, "Functions." "Functions?" I asked. "Yes, algebraic functions." While I reflected on the significance of having a young Black male scholar in mathematics education, I worried that his scholarly impact might get lost in what I thought was the narrowness of the discipline. "Are functions where your passions lie or is there something else that really matters to you?" I wondered aloud. "Well, I'm definitely concerned about Black students and their poor mathematics performance. I'm interested in the way education policy and reform are racialized," Bill replied. My face brightened and I asked, "Well, why don't you study that?" "I could study that?" Bill asked. Now I became really emboldened. "Boy, you better study that. Who else is going to do it?"

Bill used his postdoctoral year deep in the law library reading about this thing called Critical Race Theory. I remember his excitement when he shared a *Harvard Law Review* article with me by Kimberle Crenshaw (1988) entitled "Race, Reform, and Retrenchment: Transformation and Legitimation in Antidiscrimination Law." We began talking about how educational inequity could be understood through a Critical Race Theory framework. This idea signaled the beginning of our scholarly collaboration. He read widely in this field and with the help of his lawyer fiancée, Kim Cash, was able to unravel the "lawyerese." He continued to send me law review articles and before the year was out, we began collaborating on a paper (Ladson-Billings & Tate, 1995) that established our professional identities within the department and later in the field.

I often referred to Bill as "an old soul," which is a term my parents and grandparents used to describe a young person who seemed much more mature than his or her years. Bill was about 6 years older than my eldest son, yet he was wise and deliberative in ways that I could never imagine my own children to be. We grew to be close friends as well as colleagues. We had some friends and experiences in common and in the spring of 1992 Carl Grant, my husband, Charles, and I flew to Maryland to attend Bill and Kim's wedding.

Bill and I both earned tenure at the University of Wisconsin, and although it involved lots of hard work, neither of us saw earning tenure as part of an endgame. We both had larger agendas to attend to. Bill revealed to me that he was dealing with a spiritual call on his life and that he was not sure how that call was going to fit into academic life. But, as is true in almost every aspect of Bill's life, he found a way to make it work. This integration comes through clearly in his interview transcript:

> To me it's deeply spiritual and if things are not coming together, I just basically know that I can—that it's not really my work—that the work—you know, it's missionary work really. I look at it as God's work and so I—I mean, once I know that, that's when I get comforted and I just ask God, you know, [to] take over.
>
> I just ask God to take over because, you know, the Scriptures always talk about bring your little children to me.
>
> Every talk I give now I give this Scripture to people. It's been well-received in the South and not well-received when I deal with my Yankee friends [laughs]. They just don't like to deal with God at all. It's Genesis 3:21 and the reasons I give this is because for me, and here's how I want to frame it for you. I ask people over and over again, "What was the first assessment ever given?" because, you know, the world is full of all these tests now and category systems. So I ask them, "Could you tell me out of sociology where the first test was given? Can you tell me out of anthropology? Can you tell me out of economics? Psychology?" You know, you could search the annals of every one of these fields and you will not be able to talk about the first recorded assessment. That was actually given to Adam and Eve and they failed, and as educators we have to have ethics. Our practice has to be based on some set of ethics, and Adam and Eve had direct instruction. It wasn't constructivism. It wasn't project-based learning. They had direct clear instruction and they still failed. So what happened? Did they get another test? No, their needs were met immediately. [God] clothed them with these skins, and our charge as educators is that kids will fail tests, they will disappoint us, they will fall short of the mark as sure as Adam and Eve did, but the fact of the matter is, no matter how much they disappoint us, our job is to clothe them—intellectually, spiritually—with everything that we possibly have to give them.

"HE'S NOT LOOKING LIKE A PROPHET"— STORIES OF ENCOURAGEMENT (AND DISCOURAGEMENT)

Bill points to a variety of people and circumstances that shaped his career development. Although most of those were positive and encouraging, his conversation also includes some people who attempted to discourage him. In typical Bill Tate fashion, he considers all of these experiences relevant to his growth and development as a scholar. Like some of the other participants in this project, Bill did not start out seeking a career in academe. However, a series of events moved him in that direction:

> Initially as an undergraduate and [even] prior to that, my mindset was initially in thinking about a science career—and I had some negative experiences with White folks in high school [about my aspirations]. I began to think about a career more in economics because I enjoyed the math and the application. That's really where I was headed until I realized as an undergraduate that economics is a science of diminishing return.
>
> But early in my career I never thought of actually being a professor, or even being in education period was not a part of my thinking. As an undergrad, I was in econ and math and I thought I was really interested in the financial mathematical type of work. So I can't say anything in my youth was heading me toward being an academic. I can say I had excellent teaching and preparation; however, no one ever said, "Have you ever thought about being a professor?" That just never happened.

Additionally, Bill spoke of the way key moments and specific individuals caused him to think differently about academe as a career:

> I think key moment one [was] as an undergraduate. An associate dean at Northern [Illinois University], when I told him I was an econ major and wanted to go to grad school—he's the first Anglo person ever to say to me, "Why don't you take more math courses? Why don't you get a minor in math or maybe a double major?" It was a sign of encouragement. [The second key moment was when] I was fortunate enough at Northern to be tutoring. [It was] a program for Black kids where I really got a chance to [practice teaching] because I was tutoring with these kids and students—they were really peers—[and it] really gave me a chance to dig deep into the content so I got really good at it. Those are key moments, but the existence of that program, while I wasn't in it, it was important for me structurally because it allowed me to stay in school [and] helped pay for things.
>
> The third strategic point was I was offered an undergraduate TA-ship

in mathematics at Northern, which really just never happened [before]. There was such a shortage of people who could speak English [fluently] and do math. That got me into thinking about education as a career because I really enjoyed the teaching. My father's good friend and colleague who was a, you know, a PhD out of Ohio State, kept telling me over and over again that there weren't any Blacks in math and you really ought to keep going as far as you can go. That was very, very important. [A] professor, George Fair because my advisor [there] in math education, discouraged me from thinking about a PhD program. He said there were no jobs and no future in math education, and now obviously he's not looking like a prophet because [math ed] is one of the hottest areas—even in math departments—now.

So there were these people all along, in the midst of, you know, misinformation by some, who were an encouragement and said, "Continue on." Strategically, it was very important I think that a preponderance of them happened to be Black men who were positioned in education and had backgrounds in education and understood things about the education system who were encouraging and provided the kinds of references necessary to matriculate in the academic world.

"THERE ARE ONLY A FEW OF US WHO ARE IN THE POSITION TO RAISE THESE QUESTIONS"—THE ROLE OF AFRICAN AMERICAN TEACHER EDUCATORS

As I did with each of the participants in this project, I tried to determine how Bill Tate saw the role of African American teacher educators. In this part of our conversation Bill reflected on his excitement over moving back to an urban community and what he thought was possible there that was not in other more suburban and bucolic settings:

Now that I live in an urban city again, I view the kids almost like they're my own and the questions I raise in my research are the questions I would raise if I were trying to understand the environment that my own children were in. I've come to realize that there are only a few of us who are in the position to raise these questions and to have a forum for articulating them either in writing in academic code or the more public intellectual way of writing for newspapers and making comments to newspaper people about the experiences of Black children. So I see it as—I'm almost like an elected representative, since I came from an urban environment and largely one which was supportive for me. I see myself as an agent on behalf of those kids.

As our conversation moved toward how Bill saw his role in his particular institution, he talked about the benefits of working in a private school (as did Jackie Jordan Irvine) and the strategic moves he made as an African American scholar:

> Well, I mean, if you read the history of—first of all, most private universities are typically standoffish to the community. What I found here was that you can't worry about what the institution's reputation is. You have to garner internal resources to support the kind of efforts you want to do for people in the community and no one really gets in your way. There is no underbelly fighting against you. You simply have to line up people that have the kinds of skills and resources you need and you can make a difference.
>
> What I would like to see happen is that we develop an ongoing capacity to influence and change human resources around math, science, literacy, and urban education. I see math and literacy as critical to the education of urban youth and I think you cannot ignore the intricate nature of the urban context, and so you need people who have expertise in negotiating that. Between the four of those (math, science, literacy, urban education) I think those are the pillars that I would like to build on and be able to say we have ongoing capacity in terms of helping people to get better at those things.

THE SCHOLARLY CONTRIBUTIONS OF WILLIAM TATE

Bill Tate has to be credited with the movement known as Critical Race Theory in education. Although it is true that legal scholars have been thinking, researching, and writing in this vein since the mid-1970s and the formal organizing around the ideas generated by the Critical Race Theory scholars can be traced back to the organizing movement of the late 1980s (Delgado, 1995), no one in education wrote about Critical Race Theory until Bill and I published a paper in the *Teachers College Record* (Ladson-Billings & Tate, 1995).

Although I have alluded to this collaboration earlier in this chapter, it is important to present a more elaborate picture of this process here. Bill, who has a strong policy bent to his scholarship, was looking for a more powerful explanatory tool to make sense of the persistent inequity between Black and other children of color and their White counterparts. In our frequent conversations at work we became students of the legal literature and realized that it was exactly what we were looking for.

For weeks, Bill and I began outlining and writing the paper. Once we had a draft, we decided to do something a bit unorthodox for both of us.

Instead of sending it to a select group of colleagues and friends, we convened a department-wide colloquium, made scores of copies, and invited all of our colleagues to read and react to the paper. Every time I think about this, I realize just how bold we were. Neither of us was tenured. We were the first African Americans hired into the department in more than 20 years. And we were proposing a theory that represented a radical departure from the established educational literature.

Close to 30 people attended our colloquium. I guess we were something of a curiosity. Bill was as forceful as Nat Turner, and I was probably too naïve to consider backing out. There was a degree of tension in the air as we talked to a room full of White colleagues about the way race configures every aspect of education. To their credit, our colleagues listened attentively. They asked us hard questions and in the end, a number of them offered a series of constructive critiques about the manuscript.

Later in the year Bill and I presented the revised paper as a part of an advanced paper session at the American Educational Research Association annual meeting. Our reception there was much less cordial than that at the colloquium in our department. People accused us of elevating race over class and gender. Others saw us as betraying the principles of multiculturalism. We recognized that we had struck a nerve and needed to push on.

That summer we began yet another revision of the paper and sent it off to the *Teachers College Record*. The day we put the paper in the mail, Bill and I realized that we placing our careers on the line. We were putting race on the front burner as more than a variable to be isolated, held constant, or fed into a regression analysis. We wanted the educational community to recognize the central role of race in education. In the spring of 1995 the *Teachers College Record* published the article.

After the publication of the article, I went back to the work I was doing on culturally relevant pedagogy. However, Bill began to systematically integrate Critical Race Theory (CRT) into his work in mathematics education and educational policy. In 1997 Bill published what can only be described as the definitive chapter on Critical Race Theory and education (Tate, 1997). In this chapter he educated the field about CRT and its potential for transforming the way we think about educational equity.

At the same time Bill was writing about CRT he also began to transform the mathematics education landscape. Mathematics education is notorious for its ability to sidestep issues of equity, culture, and social justice. However, the performance of poor students and students of color in mathematics continues to lag far behind that of White, middle-class students. The conventional wisdom in the field focuses solely on the technical problems— teacher knowledge, materials, student aptitude, and preparation. Bill's work looks at the intersection of these technical issues with the macro issues of the structure and meaning of school mathematics. Often I have heard him say, "You can't learn math merely by taking a math course each semester. The high-achieving math students are taking several courses at a time—the official course in the curriculum (e.g., algebra, geometry, calculus) and the unofficial ones that are a part of the 'extra-curricula' program" (e.g., math club, chess club, computer club, math tutoring).

Bill Tate's contribution to the field invigorates the theory, practice, and policy of mathematics education. His work has introduced a generation of mathematics education scholars to the possibility of focusing their work on the principles of equity and justice.

"I'M WORKING ON HAVING A 'WE' CAREER"—BILL TATE'S PROFESSIONAL LIFE

My interview with Bill Tate took place about a year after he assumed a new post as department chair at Washington University. Clearly, he was enjoying this new role as administrator and being on a new campus. I worked to get him to think over his entire career as he responded to my questions. Many of his comments relate to the field of mathematics education and the dominant thinking.

As I did with the other participants, I asked Bill to think about the differences between his professional life and that of his White colleagues. Bill spoke eloquently about the differences he perceived:

> I would say I guess that in mathematics education the general impression I've always gotten is that many of these people were writing these papers for their own (careers). They were "me" people. It was just about them, and I really am trying to work on having a "we" career where it's about a broader set of people than just the work. It's about helping people; it's about giving them a vision for what might be possible; it's about exposing all forms of inequality and so, for me, my work is intricately tied to the people, whereas I see a lot of my colleagues who seem to write for their own self-gratification or . . . crass careerism.

Bill further elaborated the perceived differences between his work and that of his colleagues. He points out the perspective advantage that African American scholars may enjoy in working within African American communities:

> I don't think many of my colleagues, not just here but across the country—I know for a fact they do studies and they never, ever interact

with the people that they're studying. I know there are paradigmatic viewpoints on how to do work, but it strikes me that if you're a sociologist and you're studying an African American community, but you're doing it from afar, you really don't know what's going on—and I think they don't really want to know. They're gap gazing and we have an obligation to come to know and understand and bring meaning to the lives of the people there—in a genuine way.

I personally think we have a strategic advantage over (our White colleagues) because some of us come from those environments. I would categorize a lot of what goes on with (research about) Black (people) [as work done by people who] have not really had an experience where they really lived among Black people. The people who have either been grown up in the rural South or in these urban cities and really experienced it have a much deeper understanding of a cultural phenomenon.

Bill refers to African American teacher educators as "insider outsiders" who have "a great advantage in presenting authentic research." In some ways this characterization is a perfect description of life in the Big House. Having access to the academy provides African American scholars with an up-close view of the inner workings of the institution and the way rules are made and remade to include some people while excluding others. Bill's notion of creating a "we" career in the midst of a set of norms that push one toward a "me" career is both transgressive and transformative. Everything in graduate preparation sets people up to develop and advance their own careers. The notion of constructing an academic career to serve others is neither wise nor popular, but it reflects the maverick spirit that is Bill Tate's.

"IT'S GOOD TO HAVE A PERSON WHO WILL CHALLENGE YOU"— FORMS OF MENTORING AND SUPPORT

Each of the participants shared stories of his or her circle of support and mentoring. Bill Tate is unique in this project because he reflects the "younger generation" of African American teacher educators. For many years, few African Americans participated in the mainstream discourse, and those who entered the academy depended on help from White colleagues and friends and African American colleagues and friends from afar. Bill Tate is among the first generation of African American scholars who came into the academy with a significant number of African American teacher educators (and other professors of education) already in place and positioned to mentor and support his career:

Upon getting advice to go to Wisconsin from Howard Johnson, who had interviewed me for a position and *offered* me a position at Syracuse . . . he suggested that I go to Wisconsin even though he had offered me a job. At that point I [decided I] would not let him out of my life because anybody who would put you over themselves and their desire to have me there [is special].

Once I got to Wisconsin, I was very blessed to have [you], as well as Carl Grant. I think the most important structural thing that happened for me there was when we did the article for *Educational Policy* (1993), even though there wasn't math in it. It was instructive from the perspective of how you really put together a journal article, and it took advantage of some readings I had been doing in Critical Race Theory.

Writing the handbook chapter with Carl was good because I got a chance to see how he thought. The thing about it is, what most scholars don't get a chance to do is sit down with people who are really, really smart and try to figure out how they think. You know how you think, but when you can take the thinking of another person and really take the best of it and incorporate it into your own work, you really will become better, so you and Carl were vital in that—and also just the reality check.

It's good to have a person who will challenge you in some unique ways. I thought it was a genuinely supportive [thing] for the tenure process and [my assigned mentor, Walter Secada] did everything he possibly could to make sure it was a fair assessment, so [I] would include him as a person who was genuinely supportive.

As I think about the Wisconsin experience, I wouldn't call Michael Apple a mentor but would say he opened a door for me [by] inviting me to write for *Review of Research in Education*. [He may have considered it an act of mentorship] and some people might call it a gatekeeper structure but I think mentors are people who have cultural capital who can open doors and certainly he operated that way. If I look external to Wisconsin, other than Howard [Johnson], I always felt like Kofi Lomotey was there for me. He opened lots of doors for publication, you know, genuinely fair and open.

Along with talking the mentoring and support he received, it was important to discuss with Bill the support he gives, particularly since he has assumed the role of department chair at Washington University. One of the points of the Big House metaphor is to describe the way, once in the house, these scholars have worked to help transform the house and open its doors even wider. Bill's discussion about his role as a mentor pulls on his spiritual center and once again evokes thoughts of Nat Turner:

If we have legacies, I believe it's in our personal relationships with colleagues. Several years ago when AERA [the American Educational Research Association meeting] was in Seattle, I had made a conscious decision, a prayerful decision actually, I prayed about it and I wanted to go to Seattle. I wasn't interested in giving any papers. I was on leave from Wisconsin. I just asked God, if it were His will, to open me up to helping somebody and bring somebody into my life and He did that at that meeting. A young man who was a doctoral student at the time and I were giving a session, sort of a mentoring session. He just came up to me and I told him he could send me papers and call me and we would work together. I told him I would make a commitment to him if he was interested and that's just been actualized. Since that time we have been in constant communication with each other. He calls me about job opportunities, papers, publications.

I am inundated with other kinds of phone calls [from] people [who] just want to talk to me about their 5-year-plan or their 1-year-plan. I think I have a few letters . . . here, probably upwards of about 5 or 6 people that I constantly work with.

"WHEN ARE YOU GOING TO GET A REAL JOB?"—THE INVISIBLE CULTURE OF AFRICAN AMERICAN FAMILY SUPPORT

Although Bill Tate is a second-generation college graduate (his mother and father both are college graduates) and is married to a college graduate (his wife, Kimberly, earned her law degree from George Washington University and her parents are college graduates), he is the first family member to move into the academy. His family enjoyed Big House benefits but Bill is *in* the Big House. Despite the upward mobility of his family, Bill suggests that his family does not have a full picture of what he does and what his work entails:

I think my father knows what I do. I don't think a majority of them have a real understanding. I know when I was at Wisconsin, you could say you were at the number one school and all that, and it was a great research institution. I don't think they had a clue of the difference between Wisconsin and Chicago State. I think that they think you teach and you write a few things. They don't really know what you write. I don't share that kind of stuff really. I send stuff to my grandmother because she was pivotal in terms of my academic development.

[My grandmother, who was a first-grade teacher] spent an inordinate amount of time with us as kids working on grammar, working on memorizing our math facts, and taking us to the Museum of Science and Industry. She exposed us to—she lives in Hyde Park—the whole University of Chicago life. You know [she taught us] that there's this life associated with thinking. I always keep her updated with what I did. I did the same thing for my grandfather before he died. He was probably one of the smartest men I know, he didn't have a similar kind of education that my [maternal] grandmother had, but he was always tremendously supportive financially so I would send him copies of my articles and things. I sent him a copy of [my] dissertation—so that he would be a part of it.

I think that my mother . . . it's just more pride. She's come to my talks and has been really supportive in that way. They kind of know he gives talks and he writes books and maybe teaches, and a lot of them really don't know what the life of an academic is like, especially at these privileged largely White research institutions.

In addition to discussing the distance his work creates between him and his family, Bill also reflects on the very different career paths his college friends took. Most of his friends came from working-class families and, like him, represent the second generation of college-goers. According to Bill, their assessment of what he does is linked to their understanding of business models. As a young Black man, Bill knows that there are few African American males on the nation's university and college faculties. Thus he maintains relationships with a number of friends beyond the academy. None of his friends chose an academic career:

They know what I do and they tease me, [saying] "When are you going to get a real job?" But I think they understand the job I have now being [department] chair, because they know it's more of a management job and that's the world they're in. They're all largely corporate American type(s), so when I say I have a staff, they understand that, or when I say I do a budget and I deal with human resources and managing people and all that, they get that because they do that every day. The teaching part they all understand because they've all been in college classrooms. The research, they're less in tune with what that's all about.

"THERE ARE OTHERS OF US IN THIS COMMUNITY WHO KNOW YOU CAN DO IT"—TAKING ON THE CHARGE OF INTELLECTUAL LEADERSHIP

As my conversation with Bill Tate drew to a close we came back to his understanding of how his upbringing and professional development were linked to key family members and his faith tradition. Most interesting in this part of the conversation were not doctrinal tenets in Bill's religious up-bringing but rather a vision of Black maleness that was powerfully linked to faith. Early in this chapter I detailed Bill's attendance at Holy Angels and Archbishop Quigley Seminary. But it is here in our discussion of the factors that led to his professional success that those early familial nurturing and educational experiences surface:

> I really believe I am a product of, from an intellectual perspective, my grandmother. She was, in my opinion, probably best characterized as one who firmly believed that the African American was capable of the highest levels of intellectual engagement. She was probably most in line with DuBois. She clearly came out of [an] undergraduate experi-ence when she went to Hampton [University] back in the day, finished at University of Dayton, did her master's work and all that, and I don't think she got a "B" [i.e., earned all "A's"]. Her whole thing was we've got to compete at the highest level. [She would say] "Don't *think* you can really do it, [because] I *know* you can do it and there are others of us in this community who know you can do it." She had a group of teacher friends who were very, very supportive when we were young, just constantly saying, "You're smart, you can do this." They all lived in the neighborhood. It was just a thing where you start to really believe, and there was nothing that these [other] folks could tell you once [you] got to school that could turn you away from that.

Bill continued the conversation by explaining how his early education ex-periences reinforced the perspectives of his grandmother, particular the no-tions of independence and self help. This portion of the conversation moved me away from an original comparison of Bill with Marcus Garvey and his narrative of "Up you mighty race" to Nat Turner, who combined spiritual-ity with racial uplift:

> I'm also a product of a Black Catholic tradition [at my elementary school] that didn't rely upon the archdiocese for money. We made decisions based upon what was best for the Black people in our com-munity. If the archdiocese didn't want to support it, we went out and raised the revenue stream on our own, [the] children as well as the adults in that community. We were cut off from the archdiocese fund-ing for some time because of the decisions we made that were not consistent with the Chicago archdiocese.
>
> For example, [there was] an All Saints Day where [Father Clemons] basically told every teacher in the school that we were not to bring out any pictures of any White people and we needed to find some people who looked like us whom we could hold up and say these

people have made a contribution to society and we need to be more like that. That was heresy, basically, because you need to be canonized [to be] propped up on All Saints Day. You had things like pictures of St. James who was in our church taken down and [we] put up a picture of Martin Luther King, Jr. Obviously in Catholic tradition that would be very, very problematic, especially [back] in 1972–73, where today you probably could do it and it might not be—well, I don't think you could still do it in the Catholic Church, but clearly these were the kinds of things that he [Father Clemons] was doing and saying. It was a self-help tradition that I believe is consistent with African American culture. It was the notion of "Get off the government dime, get off the middle-class dime, the welfare dime, get off of the archdiocese dime and let's make a decision as men and women on our own." That was consistent with my grandmother's perspective. In combination it formed who I was.

NOTE

1. Information for this section was taken from the following resources: J. Baker, *Nat Turner: Cry Freedom in America*, Orlando, FL: Harcourt Brace, 1998; E. Foner, Ed., *Nat Turner*, Englewood Cliffs, NJ: Prentice Hall, 1971; F. R. Johnson, *The Nat Turner Slave Insurrection*, Murfreesboro, NC: Johnson, 1966.

EIGHT

Cherry A. McGee Banks

Charlotte Forten

Growing up in Philadelphia, I developed a keen sense of history. By U.S. standards Philadelphia is an old city and markers of history and the founding of the nation are everywhere. The downtown (or Center City) area is home to City Hall where William Penn stands above the building and looks out over the municipality. Several blocks to the east of City Hall lies the historic district where one can visit Independence Hall, Carpenter's Hall, and Betsy Ross's House. To the west the Benjamin Franklin Parkway intersects the orderly street grid at a 45-degree angle. Many of the city's cultural institutions line Franklin Parkway—the Franklin Institute and Planetarium, the Museum of Natural History, the Rodin Museum, the main branch of the library (the offspring of the first public library in the country founded by Benjamin Franklin), and the Philadelphia Art Museum, known throughout the world as the place where Sylvester Stallone's character Rocky ran up the steps at the end of his training regime. This is the Philadelphia most of the nation recognizes.

But, as an African American, I know another historic Philadelphia. This is the historic Black Philadelphia and its role in the liberation of Black people from chattel slavery. This is the Philadelphia of Richard Allen and Absalom Jones, African American clergy and founders of the African Methodist Episcopal (AME) Church. This is the Philadelphia of the Pennsylvania Anti-Slavery Society and William Still, the father of the Underground Railroad. This is the Philadelphia of the Free African Society, a group of free African Americans determined to serve as a mutual aid society because of their tenuous hold on the liberty the fledgling nation offered. One of the members of that society was James Forten, an inventor, an abolitionist, and one of the wealthiest Black men of the 1700s. Forten was the grandfather of Charlotte Forten, the woman whom I selected to represent the characteristics of project participant Cherry A. McGee Banks.

I had a little difficulty deciding on Charlotte Forten as someone who exemplifies the spirit and resolve I see in Cherry Banks, primarily because I also saw Phillis Wheatley as another exemplar. Wheatley, who lived a century before Forten, was an enslaved African who was kidnapped from Gambia and sold into slavery in Boston. There she displayed such a keen intelligence that her owners taught her to read and write, and she became the first African American to publish a book of poetry in America. I look upon Wheatley's intelligence and gentility and see an image of Cherry Banks. However, because Forten demonstrated those same qualities and was also a teacher, I felt she was a more logical choice.

Charlotte Forten was born in Philadelphia in 1837 to a privileged family who moved in the same social and civic circles as William Lloyd Garrison and John Greenleaf Whittier. Her mother died while she was a young girl and she was sent to live with her uncle and aunt, Robert and Harriet Purvis, in their home just outside Philadelphia. The Purvises would not allow Charlotte to attend the racially segregated schools of Philadelphia and hired private tutors for her. Later she was sent to live with another set of prominent Black abolitionists, Charles and Sarah Remond of Salem, Massachusetts, where she graduated from Higginson Grammar School in 1855. Charlotte Forten became the first African American teacher ever hired by the Salem schools. However, she developed a stronger commitment to the cause of freedom and became a teacher to the Black children on St. Helena Island, South Carolina, in the midst of the Civil War. As the Union forces occupied both St. Helena and Port Royal islands, the White owners fled and left the formerly enslaved Africans. Under the auspices of Philadelphia's Port Royal Relief Association, Charlotte Forten was sent to teach the newly liberated Blacks.

Charlotte quickly learned how her privileged background and upbringing distanced her from the poor Gullah-speakers of the Sea Islands. Despite contemporary dramatic presentations (see Crane, 1985) of Forten's life that perhaps suggest her inability to bridge the social class divide with the people, her own words are more instructive as she describes her work with the children:

> I never before saw children so eager to learn, although I had had several years' experience in the New England schools. Coming to school is a constant delight and recreation to them. They come here as other children go to play. The older ones, during the summer, work in the fields from early morning until eleven or twelve o'clock, and then come into school, after their hard toil in the hot sun, as bright and as anxious to learn as ever. (Forten, 1864, p. 588)

Today, Forten's most enduring legacies are the diaries she left that cover the years 1854 and 1885 to 1892. From these diaries we learn that she was an intelligent, cultured woman who read and wrote poetry, attended lectures, worked as a teacher, and was an active part of the antislavery movement.

Indeed, Forten was a woman of privilege. She also was a woman of social commitment. Her stately demeanor and quiet determination make her a perfect model for Cherry A. McGee Banks.

"MY JOURNEY HAS NOT BEEN A DIRECT ONE"—CHERRY BANKS' EARLY PROFESSIONAL LIFE

Of all the participants in this volume, Cherry Banks is the one with whom my relationship is most indirect. My first recollection of meeting Cherry was at a National Council for the Social Studies conference. I had known Cherry's husband, James A. Banks, professionally for many years, and as is true of many professionals, we tend to forget that what makes their lives work is the support systems of spouses, partners, family, friends, church, and civic associations. In Jim's case, Cherry is a constant support and colaborer in the work of multicultural education.

A major part of Cherry's responsibility in their early years was raising their children and supporting Jim as he became one of the few African American tenure track faculty on a large research university campus. But she was also preparing herself to enter the academy. Just as I described my relationship with Cherry as indirect, she describes her route to the academy in a similar way:

> I think my journey has not been a direct one. It's been very indirect—kind of like a tumbling ribbon with periods of being up and periods of being down and kind of flowing but not ever directly linking things.
>
> A lot of my early work involved research and writing. For example, when I worked as a curriculum specialist in a local school district, I frequently researched issues we confronted and shared my findings in the form of informal papers with my colleagues and supervisors. I continue to use those same skills today in my work in the academy, and so being in the academy, worked very nicely for me.

Cherry's educational preparation is suggestive of the "tumbling ribbon" as she made her way to the academy. She received very interdisciplinary training and used a variety of social science disciplines to create her career:

> I studied the social sciences, specifically psychology, anthropology, and sociology, and so those disciplines became a lens for looking at

the world. I went on to get a master's degree in counseling where I
built on the psychology base and then ultimately went into educational leadership, which is also very interdisciplinary and pulls on a lot
of literature in psychology. So that's probably the thread that weaves
through all of it.

Cherry's early professional work was in counseling and although this
work was not directly related to the professorate, she recognized that the skills
she used in counseling were foundational to the work she would later do:

I saw myself doing work as a professional counselor, and that's the
type of direct work that I did immediately. But again kind of coupled
with that, during the time I was working on the counseling degree, as
well as after completing it, I was always writing and always involved
in doing research of one sort or another. So even though it wasn't directly related to thinking about my going into the academy—which
didn't occur in terms of something that I wanted to do or was interested in doing until much, much later—I was really laying the foundation
for the kinds of skills and knowledge that would be appropriate for a
person in higher education.

As other participants in this project found, the true beginning of a career in
the academy starts well before one imagines it. It begins in the hopes, dreams,
aspirations, and examples of significant people in our lives. In Cherry's case,
the significant people were parents and family members:

They start right at the very beginning with family and the early so-
cialization that I received from my mother, father, and grandmother.
My grandmother was very involved in the Civil Rights movement
and thought it was essential for all of her grandchildren to also be
involved, and so, among other things, she started a youth branch of
the NAACP and we were all required to be members. While that had
some aspects to it that were probably resisted simply because it was
something that was required of us, it provided a wonderful foundation for learning about the importance of equity and also learning
about the importance of volunteer work in the community. One of the
things that my grandmother said and I've really embraced is that to
those who have been given much, much is expected. The idea that if
you have ability, if you have position, if you have resources, those are
things that are really blessings for you and you shouldn't think of those
things as belonging only to you. You have to give back to the community. She did that on a daily basis throughout her life, and I observed
her doing it, and that was a very important lesson for me.

I am struck by the similarities between Cherry's story and those of the other participants (as well as my own) with regard to the ways parents and family members insisted on the distribution of whatever talents or resources that any individual manifested. The fostering of reciprocity and mutuality appears in literature on African cultural norms (see Boykin, 1979; King & Mitchell, 1990/1995) and represents a normative pattern in African American childrearing. One can see how these values are displayed in Cherry's early upbringing:

> My mother was kind of a southern lady and did not work outside of the home until I was a teenager, and [she] basically taught me a lot about caring and about supporting a family and about being there for other people. My father taught me the value of hard work. He worked, frankly, 7 days a week and was always doing something. [He] got us up very early in the morning and was always focused on completing a task. He taught all of us, even though we were girls, that we could do basically anything, and we were involved in doing a lot of things that girls didn't do in those days, such as mowing the lawn [laughs], washing cars, going fishing with him, and things of that nature.

"I HAVE THIS . . . ABSOLUTELY IMPOSSIBLE DREAM"—CHERRY BANKS'S VISION OF TEACHER EDUCATION

Although Cherry refers to a rather indirect path to the teacher education professorate, she does see a straight line between who she is and the work she has chosen to do. As other project members have indicated, the line between personal and professional becomes quite blurred when one's work is linked with issues of social justice and equity. Cherry articulated her connection as follows:

> I see a direct connection. The work that I do is very much tied to my understanding of myself as an African American woman who has African American children. I always thought, being kind of a child of the 60s, that the issues that we were addressing in the 60s would not be issues that my children would have to address. And in many ways the issues have changed, but in some significant ways they've stayed the same, and so the work that I'm involved in with respect to multicultural education is very much tied to my understanding of the importance of changing our society to make it better for people who look like me, as well as the entire society. I see those linkages being very direct.

Cherry points out that her choice to teach at the University of Washington, Bothell Campus, is one that allowed her to begin with a clean slate and build from the ground up. Rather than cope with frozen institutional practices and spend time trying to convince colleagues to try new things, she could function as one of the architects of a new way of thinking:

> I've always worked in predominately White institutions and have frequently been the only African American in the institution, or one of a handful. The issues that I'm concerned with are issues that are articulated by a range of people in those institutions, and so I don't feel as if I'm isolated in terms of my concerns. But, in terms of the kind of demographic overlay of the institutions, they are quite, quite different from me, from my kind of personal background.
>
> The reason I was interested in going to Bothell was because it would provide me with an opportunity to do something that was unique, and that was to build a program where there would not be limitations on what could be done. We had a clean slate and were building an institution from the ground up, and that has been a very exciting, and, I think in many ways, a very rewarding though challenging experience.

Cherry sees her work as an opportunity to bring White prospective teachers to a deeper and more complex understanding of their role in educating all students, not just students who look just like them. At this point of our interview she talked passionately and in detail about her work in teacher education:

> I have this absolutely, I think in some ways, impossible dream [laughs], in some ways what I believe is the only dream that is going to be . . . one that is going to be possible for all of us, and that is, through teacher education, we help students to become more effective and capable in working with the full range of students in their classrooms. That simple statement takes on very complex elements in that frequently the teachers I work with are teachers who are middle-class and White and have had very little experience working with students of color and have had very little experience grappling with the kinds of issues that I raise. For example, I frequently will ask students about the first time that they realized that everybody in the world wasn't basically just like them. And then I talk a bit about how I came to that understanding, and frequently students will say that they came to that understanding maybe as teenagers, adults, or it's a long way down the line, and that is so completely different in terms of [the experience

of] most people of color—and particularly if you're upwardly mobile. So we enter into discussions where we can talk about those kinds of things and how limited their experiences have been as a result of some sense of encapsulation that they've been a part of. One of the things that I try to do with students is to help them to see themselves within a broader context of the world so that they see the importance of what we're [you and I] talking about, because in many cases they're not going to go to schools where there will be large numbers of people of color. They will be in schools pretty much like the schools they attended. The kinds of issues that we're talking about are not issues that are limited to a particular group of students but are important for essentially everyone. And helping students come to that understanding has been a very difficult kind of thing to do. [It is] not something that they easily understand in terms of the benefits for them, how to do it, or how to translate it into their own experience. One of the things that I've come to understand over time is how [they feel]. I try to put myself in their position because the one immediate kind of response might be that they're the same, or they're not interested, or that in some ways they're hostile to the kinds of ideas you're talking about. But what I have come to understand is that they really have a very difficult time cognitively understanding what these issues are, and then what they should do about them.

THE SCHOLARLY CONTRIBUTIONS OF CHERRY A. MCGEE BANKS

For more than three decades Cherry A. McGee Banks has contributed a number of important publications to the field of multicultural education. Her scholarship and research primarily focus on factors related to school improvement, such as curriculum and instruction, and on factors related to educational leadership. Survey and archival research are the two primary methodologies used in her research. Cherry's scholarship has resulted in a continuous record of publications that began with her master's thesis, in she which used content analysis to examine the treatment of Blacks on popular television programs. A 1977 article based on that work was published in the research section of *Social Education*. It provides a model of a scientific content analysis that is still used by students today. In "Intellectual Leadership and the Influence of Early African American Scholars on Multicultural Education," an article published in *Educational Policy*, Cherry Banks (1995) develops the concept of "meta-narratives," which she constructs with the master narrative of the mainstream culture. Her conceptualization of the meta-narrative and the master narrative has been influential and important to the field.

Cherry's work on the history of the intergroup education movement is perhaps her most original and important contribution to the field. The intergroup education movement was an antecedent to the multicultural education movement. Intergroup educators worked from the 1920s to the 1950s to reduce prejudice and misunderstanding among ethnic and racial groups by developing curriculum materials, approaches, techniques, and ways to mobilize school and community resources to improve human relations and foster intergroup understanding. Cherry has been working on constructing a history of the intergroup education movement for several years. She made a series of presentations at AERA on intergroup education and published chapters on it in *Multicultural Education, Transformative Knowledge, and Action* (Banks, 1996) and in the second edition of the *Handbook of Research on Multicultural Education* (Banks & Banks, 2004). Her book on the intergroup education movement, *Improving Multicultural Education: Lessons From the Intergroup Education Movement*, was published in the fall of 2004 by Teachers College Press.

An important goal of her work on intergroup education is to connect present-day educators with their predecessors who faced many of the same problems they are struggling with today. By drawing on the past to enhance and extend their knowledge about educating students in a diverse society, educators can enlarge their thinking and practice and gain a better understanding of ways to reduce student prejudice and improve the self-esteem and image of students from diverse ethnic, racial, and religious groups.

"I'M BEGINNING TO SEE THINGS THAT I'D NEVER SEEN BEFORE"— CHERRY BANKS'S IMPACT ON THE PROFESSION

Because the name Banks has come to be associated with all things multicultural and all things multicultural have come to be associated with James A. Banks, Cherry Banks's contribution to the field has not been as prominent as it should be. When Cherry and I talked, she spoke primarily about her impact on the students she has taught. Much of Cherry's work has been produced collaboratively with James, and as she talks about teaching, she talks about her collaborative work with faculty colleagues:

> They [the students] had about four different courses, all dealing with aspects of multicultural education, and the entire program, because the faculty in this program are very committed to issues of equity, and all of us came from a foundations perspective. My colleagues had backgrounds in educational anthropology and sociology and grounded their teaching in that subject matter perspective. So in all of

our classes we raised questions that pushed students and helped them to think about issues and concerns that they would not have necessarily thought about, and they didn't simply get that perspective in [some other] courses. It made it so much easier, because when they would come to my classes, they were ready to think about those issues in a deeper way, and when they went into other classes, they continued to think about them and ultimately recognize how the faculty's commitment to social justice linked all of the classes in the program together. As a result of that, students were able to broaden their thinking about the issues. In order to move forward in the program, they had to relinquish or at least pull away from the familiar as they would form a broader understanding of the world around them. They would say things like, "This has been the most powerful learning experience I've had in my entire life, K–12, college, the entire thing," or, you know, "I'm beginning to see things that I'd never seen before."

"AFRICAN AMERICAN STUDENTS IN ALL THE DIFFERENT PROGRAMS WOULD COME TO ME"—WORKING IN WHITE INSTITUTIONS

Like all of the project participants, Cherry Banks has experienced what it means to be in the minority. In Cherry's case, she has worked at two institutions where she was the only African American on the faculty. Both at Seattle University and at the University of Washington-Bothell, Cherry has had to depend on White colleagues to provide the intellectual and institutional support to help her advance and earn tenure and promotion. Instead of trying to seek out individuals for support, Cherry sought to create a team of colleagues. Like Charlotte Forten, she seemed determined to create a kind of institutional change that would yield results that had more than personal benefit. Forten worked with the women of the Anti-Slavery Society to help them recognize the possibilities that lay in the freedmen, and in many ways Cherry's very presence at these institutions served a similar function:

I'd say almost the entire faculty [at Seattle University] served as mentors. It was a wonderful place to begin my teaching in higher education because there were so many excellent teachers there. It was also a very caring and supportive environment and a lot of positive kinds of things were going on there. There was a particular person who was identified as my mentor, but it was really more of a whole department kind of thing.

I think probably the most important thing that it [being at Seattle University] did was it provided me an opportunity to do some reality checking—in terms of teaching—but I also got the wonderful mentoring of Margaret McGuire. She put me on several NCSS committees and gave me access to some important professional connections.

Because she was the only African American faculty member at both instittions in which she worked, Cherry did not have an opportunity to serve as an on-site mentor to other African American faculty members. Instead she turned her mentoring activities toward African American students. She understood the importance of just offering a friendly face and an approachable demeanor to students who feel lost in the midst of a sea of White faces:

> I think [I was probably a mentor] more in terms of students both at Seattle U. as well as the Bothell campus of the university because I was the only African American faculty member. I think that they would say that I was a mentor in terms of providing them with support in the sense that there was somebody there they could talk to. One of the interesting things about Bothell is that African American students in all the different programs come [to] talk to me. They'll see me in the hall and they'll come by my office and just talk. I've had students in other programs who invited me to activities that they've been a part of outside the university. One student left Bothell, went away to another institution, and when he graduated, he sent me a graduation invitation . . . so I think that there is a sense of comfort having someone on the faculty who looks like them. Frequently they will bring questions and concerns to me about what's happening in their programs and how students and faculty respond to them. In that sense I think I've been able to help.

"WE MANAGED TO PULL OURSELVES TOGETHER AND TO SURVIVE AND TO MOVE ON"—THE INFLUENCE OF AFRICAN AMERICAN CULTURE ON CHERRY BANKS'S WORK

Although Cherry Banks has spent her entire professional career as a teacher educator in the Pacific Northwest, her African American heritage continues to provide her with support and serves as a resource for her thinking and working in teacher education. Once again, listening to her made me think of Charlotte Forten and the incredible diversity within the African American community. Forten was a learned person in an era when most people, Black or White, were illiterate. She came from a privileged family of shipbuilders and entrepreneurs. However, she demonstrated a commitment to the masses of Black people who were struggling from the vestiges of chattel slavery and the lack of access to education that would allow them to participate in a changing American economy.

Cherry Banks did not emerge from a privileged background, but she did have access to the kind of family roots that stressed commitment to the masses of Black people and to democracy as a way of life for all people. Cherry's father worked as a tool-and-die maker in Michigan for the Clark Equipment Company. Cherry describes her father's employer as "a very oppressive environment" but one through which she learned "the importance of perseverance and continuing in the face of opposition." She saw her father confront discrimination at work but continue on, and that persistence and perseverance gave her an important perspective on what was expected of her as an African American. When I asked her what she saw as the most important aspects of African American culture that have been significant in her professional success, she responded:

> I think probably the most important is resilience. I think one element in the African American cultural that has allowed us to be here today and tell the story is that we, under very adverse circumstances, managed to pull ourselves together and to survive and to move on and to provide that foundation for the next generation, and that's what I think is probably the most important for me. I always, whenever I run into a difficult circumstance or a setback—I don't think of failure. I think, "Hey, well this is going to require rethinking and a new approach, but we're going to continue."

In addition to stressing the influence of her father and his perseverance, Cherry again referred to her grandmother and her notion of community and cultural responsibility:

> I [always] go back to the statement that I mentioned earlier by my grandmother—the idea [that] to those who are given much, much is expected, and while I'm not suggesting that I am privileged, in a kind of global way, I think that there are elements in my life that suggest that I have something I can give back to the community, and in that sense my grandmother's statement represents something that is a slogan in my life. I think that it called my attention to the importance of volunteering. So whatever I'm doing, however I'm situated in terms of my work, I always find time to volunteer because I think that is really essential. I think that it's important for me to be connected to the larger institutional issues that are going on within the university because those are issues that will shape the ability of faculty to be able to do the kinds of things that they want to do. So in that sense because I have a vision, and an understanding of these larger issues, I have to then position myself so that I can influence the direction that they take.

"I HAVE HAD WONDERFUL OPPORTUNITIES PRESENTED TO ME"— CARVING AN INDEPENDENT SCHOLARLY IDENTITY

Of all of the participants in this project, Cherry A. McGee Banks holds the unique position of being married to one of the leading scholars in her field. Indeed, as I conceived of this project, I initially considered having James Banks as a participant. However, as we talked, Jim insisted that he was sufficiently distant from teacher education to preclude him from being an ideal candidate. As we talked about the project, Jim and I both agreed that Cherry would make an excellent participant. She fit the criterion of being an African American teacher educator whom I have known over many years. But, because of her unique status as spouse and partner to Jim, I felt compelled to ask her about how she was able to craft a separate intellectual identity. Once again, echoes of Charlotte Forten emerged as I developed Cherry's portrait. Forten was both from a prominent family and later married a prominent abolitionist minister, Francis Grimke. As our interview concluded, I felt compelled to ask Cherry the question about developing her separate and distinct identity:

> I think that I have really been very privileged to have the opportunity to work so closely with someone who is the leading figure, or certainly one of the leading figures, in this field, and as a result of that, I have had wonderful opportunities presented to me and hopefully I have been able to take advantage of a lot of those opportunities. The challenge is always, when you're in a situation like that, to be identified as a person in her own right, and that has always been a challenge. It's been an ongoing challenge. Jim and I actually joke about it because even when we write things independent of each other as well as [when] we write together, sometimes things I've written will be attributed to Jim, and things he's written will be attributed to me. So we'll laugh and we'll say, "Well now you've become coauthor of [a particular piece]" or I'll laugh and say, "Well, Jim, now you've gotten credit for this." That happens all the time and basically it's not an issue for me. It's not something that I'm concerned with at all, because I know that's just a kind of reality that I have to deal with, and it will always be an issue. There are people who feel that I shouldn't write with Jim because we're married. We married at a time when women tended to take their husband's name. We've been married (more than 35 years). If I had maintained my maiden name, some of this would not be an issue. Many people in higher education are married and work together and write together but they have

different names, and if you don't know they're married, then it's generally not an issue. But that's not the case for us, and so I basically feel that there have been wonderful opportunities that have been afforded to me and I prefer to focus on those activities—those opportunities—and yes, there are some challenges that go along with the opportunities.

As I completed my interview with Cherry A. McGee Banks, I was struck by the degree to which the interview process created a new level of intimacy. I have known Cherry for many years as "Jim Banks's wife." Even with my own feminist leanings, I was not oblivious to the large shadow Jim's fame cast over Cherry and her work. However, the process of dialogue with her provided me a unique opportunity to inquire about her work in the academy and the way she has composed her life (Bateson, 1989).

Our conversation underscored the myriad ways that Black people represent themselves and Black interests in the academy. Her quiet dignity and perseverance brought forth yet another iteration of participation in the Big House without total capitulation to it.

NINE

Lisa Delpit

Lagniappe

In Louisiana there is a Creole term, *lagniappe,* that refers to an extra or unexpected gift or benefit. One could think of lagniappe as something akin to a baker's dozen. The custom of giving lagniappe is prevalent throughout Southern Louisiana and Mississippi. As I conceptualized this final chapter I realized that it contains some lagniappe. In addition to trying to synthesize what I learned from this research project, I include aspects of the life story of another scholar who was as eager to participate in the project as I was to have her. Unfortunately, we could not arrange enough interview time to do a full chapter exploration.

Lisa Delpit is one of the people I most wanted to include in this project. Lisa's life parallels my own in busyness and overall "academic chaos." We seem to always be trying to farm off speaking engagements and consultancies on each other. I regularly receive phone calls that begin, "Lisa Delpit told me to contact you," and I regularly say to some anonymous voice on the end of the phone, "Have you tried Lisa Delpit?"

During my visit to Atlanta to interview Jacqueline Jordan Irvine, I also arranged to interview Lisa Delpit. Unfortunately, Lisa's daughter Maya was ill on the day I had planned to do the interview. Although Lisa graciously offered to slip away for a few hours, I had enough sense to know that moms belong with sick children. For the next couple of years we kept trying to find time to do the interview.

Finally, we agreed to try to do part of the interview electronically, but again responsibilities conspired against us. I decided that I needed to get on with the project and would have to forego the Delpit interview. However,

Lisa Delpit is one of those people about whom much is already written, and I have known her for more than 15 years, so I can at least put some of that information in the context of this larger study.

As I did with several of the other participants, I had difficulty deciding on a single African American heroine or legend on which to base my profile of Lisa Delpit. I wavered between Anna Julia Cooper and Queen Mother Moore. I was drawn to Queen Mother Moore because of the similarity of their backgrounds—both from Louisiana and both fiery spirits. I also thought that the commanding presence of Queen Mother Moore foreshadowed a similar presence in Lisa. If you have ever attended a lecture or presentation by Lisa, you know that she fills a room both literally and figuratively. I remember a visit she made to Wisconsin where we needed to open up an overflow room and broadcast the lecture on closed-circuit television. One of my European American colleagues looked at me and exclaimed, "This is not a lecture, it's a happening!"

However, as striking as Queen Mother Moore was as a historical figure and activist, I think Anna Julia Cooper's pioneering scholarship, racial uplift discourse, and feminist work commingle to create a wonderful portrait of the Lisa Delpit I have come to know. Because this final chapter is indeed lagniappe, I will not provide a full discussion of either Anna Julia Cooper or Lisa Delpit. Rather, I will underscore some of the reasons why these women offer us a new vision of who and how to be in the academy.

WHO WAS ANNA JULIA COOPER?

Anna Julia Cooper is a foundational figure among Black feminists in America (Lemert & Bhan, 1998). She was born in North Carolina sometime around 1858 and died in Washington, D.C., in 1964. Her scholarly career spans almost 50 years and begins about 20 years after Reconstruction and continues into and beyond the Harlem Renaissance of the 1920s. Among her colleagues and contemporaries were Mary Church Terrell, Ida B. Wells Barnett, and Charlotte Forten. Cooper was an accomplished intellectual and teacher of the classics, modern and ancient languages, literature, mathematics, and the sciences. She actually functioned as a teaching assistant at the age of 10 in mathematics at St. Augustine College in Raleigh, North Carolina, and continued teaching until she was well into her 80s. After Cooper had taught high school for more than 35 years, her translation of *Le Pèlerinage de Charlemagne* from old to modern French brought her professional accolades as she was doing graduate work at Columbia University. At the age of 66, Anna Julia Cooper completed her doctoral thesis at the Sorbonne on French attitudes toward slavery during the French Revolution. But Cooper is probably best known to American readers because of a speech delivered in 1886 when she was just 2 years out of Oberlin College, 27 years old, and speaking before a meeting of an all male, African American clergy. Cooper's speech, "Womanhood: A Vital Element in the Regeneration and Progress of a Race" (which was published as the first chapter of her book *A Voice from the South*, 1892/1988), must have incensed her audience when she said what have become famous words:

> Only the Black Woman can say "when and where I enter, in the quiet, undisputed dignity of my womanhood, without violence and without suing or special patronage, then and there the whole Negro race enters with me." (quoted in Lemert & Bhan, 1998, p. 63)

Lemert and Bhan (1998) describe Anna Julia Cooper's way as "direct, eloquent, ever dignified, never obsequious; thus, disturbing, but convincing" (p. 7). Anyone who has spent any time with Lisa Delpit will immediately recognize the similarities in spirit and personality.

WHO IS LISA DELPIT AND WHY ARE THEY SAYING THOSE THINGS ABOUT HER?

I am one of those people who encountered Lisa Delpit the person before meeting Lisa Delpit the scholar and trying to interpret her through her scholarship. Sometime in the late 1980s, a group of African American teacher educators was convened at Stanford University to speak to concerns we had raised individually about new protocols for assessing teaching competence. As I think back to that meeting, it was a pretty impressive group, although few of us had any national reputation or profile at that time. Among the scholars[1] were Joyce King, Etta Hollins, Michele Foster, Sharon Nelson Barber, Lisa Delpit, and I. Because Joyce King and I lived in the area, we used this 2 to 3-day meeting as an opportunity to get together outside of the official agenda to talk and think about what was happening to Black teachers and Black schoolchildren and what we could do about them.

That evening we were talking at Joyce King's home. Because I had spent the entire day at the official Stanford meeting, I was obligated to pick up my maternal duties and brought my then-toddler daughter with me.[2] I remember clearly how smitten Lisa was with Jessica. Although she was engaged in the conversation, her eyes never left my busy, active child, and often her arms reached out as well. I like to think this encounter helped to seal the deal when some years later Lisa became the proud adoptive parent of toddler Maya.

After reading Lisa's essay, "Skills and Other Dilemmas of a Progressive Black Educator" (1986), I contacted her to let her know that I recognized the school in which she taught. She laughed with surprise when I correctly identified it. I recall telling her there was only one school in Philadelphia with that population makeup, and her analysis of what was happening to Black children at the school was right on target.

Lisa's sharp critique of so-called progressive pedagogy that produced less success among Black children than so-called traditional methods earned her a strange array of allies and enemies, but like Anna Julia Cooper she was not about to back down. Two years later she published another essay in the *Harvard Educational Review* (Delpit, 1988) that firmly established her as a brilliant writer and as someone willing to speak truth to power.

Lisa's academic pedigree is impeccable, and those who would challenge her authority to speak and write as she does are treading on very thin ice. A graduate of Antioch College in Ohio where progressive ideology and radical approaches reigned, Lisa went on to complete master's and doctoral studies at Harvard University's Graduate School of Education. Before pursuing graduate studies, she taught school in Philadelphia where she saw firsthand that the "progressive" strategies she had learned in teacher education did not work for all the students, particularly the African American students.

Later Lisa spent a year in Papua, New Guinea, investigating indigenous approaches to education and seeing firsthand what she already knew—that people of color were capable of educating their children. Finally, she spent time in Alaska where she worked as an assistant professor of teacher education at the University of Alaska. When I met her, she had just turned down an offer from a major research university and was about to pursue a unique opportunity with a large urban school district. She also wanted to be settled and stable somewhere to demonstrate to an adoption agency that she would be a fit parent. Shortly after making that decision, Lisa was awarded the prestigious MacArthur Fellowship, commonly known as "the genius award." The award gave her incredible flexibility and made the new addition in her life, baby Maya, inevitable.

Although this truncated version of Lisa's story makes her life and career seem especially rosy, it glosses over the vilification Lisa has suffered from scholars and classroom teachers alike. "Skills and Other Dilemmas" plunged her right in the middle of the "reading wars," akin to being a police officer in the midst of a domestic dispute. Both sides were already fighting each other, and when Lisa tried to bring some sanity and coherence to the discussion, both seemed to turn on her. Her second *Harvard Education Review* essay, "The Silenced Dialogue," created a firestorm among teachers. Almost everywhere I went I heard, "Is she saying White teachers can't teach Black children?" or more pointedly, "Delpit is saying that White teachers can't teach Black children." That is not what she was saying, but she was questioning the degree to which we should be reinforcing a notion that Black people do not know anything about educating their own children and that

White people know everything about teaching them. It was a plainspoken, eloquently argued treatise and it went a long way in pushing my thinking and my work. She was a genius!

"WILL IT HELP THE SHEEP?"—LISA DELPIT'S CONTRIBUTION TO TEACHER EDUCATION

Although all of the scholars in this project are committed to teachers and teaching, Lisa Delpit has pursued her career in a way that especially highlights the two. She has accepted positions that give priority to working in schools with teachers. After leaving Morgan State University in Baltimore where she located her urban education center, Lisa became the Benjamin E. Mays Chair of Urban Educational Leadership at Georgia State University. This position required her to spend half of her time as a traditional faculty member and the other half as an "in-the-trenches school reformer" (Viadero, 1996).

In her *Education Week* interview (Viadero, 1996), she reiterates something she said to me as I was beginning the study on successful teachers of African American children, "We must keep the perspective that people are experts in their own lives." This theme has helped to direct my research and guide my methodology for almost 20 years.

Because Lisa is so gifted with words, I am ever mindful of the many things she has said over the years that challenge and inspire my work. On a panel with her at a professional meeting, I recall her telling this story:

> Two anthropologists went to do research on a Navajo reservation. One of the two wanted to take photographs of the setting and asked a Navajo elder if he could take pictures of the sheep. "Will it hurt the sheep?" the elder asked. "Oh, no. It won't hurt the sheep," the anthropologist replied with a smile of confidence on his face. He believed that his answer meant he would have no trouble gaining all the access he needed. However, another question came from the elder. "Will it help the sheep?" To this question, the puzzled anthropologist replied, "No, it won't help the sheep." The elder then asked, "Then why do it?"

Lisa posed the same question to educational researchers. If it isn't going to help them, why do it? This approach to teaching and teacher education is clear in Lisa's work. She is not interested in doing work that won't help. She has eschewed the so-called high-powered research university scene in favor of working in institutions that afford her the opportunity to work directly with teachers, parents, and community members. In many ways, Lisa is as close to a Black public intellectual as we have in education. She speaks to a wide audience in commonsense terms about the things people care about—

their children, their education, and their communities.

Like Anna Julia Cooper's, Lisa Delpit's primary focus is on the children. Cooper opened her home to foster children, the well-known abolitionist family, the Grimke's, and the working poor of the District of Columbia (Lemert, 1998). When asked to describe her vocation in a 1930 survey, Cooper responded, "The education of neglected people" (Lemert, 1998, p. 13).

Although Lisa's work is generally activist, it is not solely practice-based. In the "Silenced Dialogue" she introduces readers to the notion of the "culture of power" (Delpit, 1988) that has become an important conceptual rubric for teachers and prospective teachers to use to understand the way marginalized students have limited access to social benefits. By naming this culture of power, Lisa points out to many teachers (White and people of color) that although they may not be personally implicated in acts of racism and discrimination, their ready access to this culture of power makes them morally and ethically responsible for explicitly instructing students in the ways of the mainstream. More directly than any other scholar in education, Lisa Delpit has made it clear that Black children and other children of color must become bicultural if they are to develop the skills to attack injustice and inequity.

Among African American preachers there is a category known as "a preacher's preacher." This is the person whom other preachers run to hear. This person is a wise wordsmith who is seen as "anointed" and destined to carry forth the gospel. Theologians such as James Cone or Gardner C. Taylor fit this category. They are not necessarily the most flamboyant or heads of the largest congregations. They are known for their insights into both this world and the spiritual realm. They touch our souls and activate our minds. Lisa Delpit is a "teacher educator's teacher educator." We read her work and listen carefully to her because she tells us things not just about teaching and teacher education. She also tells us about ourselves.

JOURNEYING WITH AFRICAN AMERICAN TEACHER EDUCATORS—
WHAT IT ALL MEANS

One of the things my graduate students most dread is what has come to be known as the "so what" question. This happens after they have elegantly described their problem statement, catalogued the relevant literature, made their hypotheses, explained their research design and data collection procedures, analyzed the data, and reported their findings. At that point I look at them and give a deadpan stare accompanied by the words, "So what?"

I do not ask this question to be mean, and I certainly do not ask it in the middle of a dissertation defense. But, at some point during the many conferences we have, I raise the "so what" question. In other words, I want them to be able to articulate what the point of their work is. What difference does it make for us to know what you have found out in the course of this research? It is the one question that puts the most convivial of my students on the defensive. "What do you mean 'so what'?" is the question I can see swirling about their brains and traveling across the expression on their faces even if they never speak it aloud. It is a hard question and often the last thing many researchers ask themselves.

Now the question is turned on me—so what? It is no kinder or gentler when I ask it of myself. I feel a lot like my students. I wanted to do this project because of some deep existential need. I wanted to be able to justify my own work and to be able to say it was valuable. I had a great time doing this work. I got to speak in depth and spend time with some of the people I most trust, respect, and like. And I did learn a lot about them and from them, but does this answer the "so what" question?

Had I stayed with my original research plan, it is likely I would have produced a very conventional text about the challenges faced by African American teacher educators. I believe such a text may have satisfied all of the traditional canons of educational research. I would have had a problem statement, a review of the literature, a set of hypotheses, a research design and methodology, and a set of conclusions. I may even have offered some important implications for practice and further study. But the significant departure I took—to look more carefully at each individual in relation to important figures in our history and culture—placed me in an entirely different research space.

I take courage from the work of Yvonna Lincoln and Norman Denzin (1998), who argue that doing qualitative research in the "fifth moment"[3] is always fraught with tensions. Such tensions address six fundamental issues: grappling with positivism and postpositivism in the midst of self-critique and self-appraisal, crises of representation, crises of legitimation, the emergence of multiple voices, the movement between the scientific and sacred, and the influence of technology. In the remaining pages I address how this project has helped me make sense of the challenges of doing research in the "fifth moment."

Positivism and Postpositivism Versus Self-Critique and Self-Appraisal

This tension is probably the easiest for me to resolve. In all of my work I have argued about the limits of positivist paradigms in capturing the complexity that is education research. To that end I endorse Bruner's (1993) notions that:

> The qualitative researcher is not a neutral, objective, politically disinterested party who stands outside the text;
> The qualitative researcher is historically and locally situated, i.e., a human actor in a human drama;
> Meaning is multiple and political and every account includes politics. (p. 1)

Because of the broad participation of the society in education, it is impossible to tell one story about schooling and education. It is a multi-layered, multidisciplinary enterprise, and we must use multiple lenses to understand what is transpiring. There are aspects of the work that are amenable to positivist research. I happen not to be invested in the questions such research answers. I am less concerned with how many standard deviations certain groups of students fall from the norm than with what the underlying social conditions that produce such disparities look like. I am not suggesting that the former question is not valuable—I need it to raise my own questions. However, I have made a conscious decision to ask fewer "what" questions and more "how" and "why" questions. This move away from positivism is linked to my own decision to be more self-critical.

In the course of this project I was forced to move back and forth between my understanding of African American teacher educators and those of the project participants. Why were there convergences and divergences in our perspectives? What was I attempting to overlay on the project that did not belong there? What was I holding back that should have been more present?

Crises of Representation

This project is closely tied to crises of representation both external and internal. The external ones are alluded to in Chapter 1 where I reference the limited studies on teacher education and the total absence of studies on African American teacher educators. What is said about teaching and teacher education rarely includes the voices (whether they are in agreement or dissent) of African American teacher educators.

Methodologically, this project represents a crisis of representation because of the way I chose to offer the portraits of the participants to you. I selected historical or mythical personalities that seemed to reflect particular essences of the participants. They did not contribute to this decision. Although I asked all of the participants to read and react to their chapters, they were not free to say, "I don't want to be represented by this person." I chose aspects of their personalities that were revealed to me as a part of our working and personal relationships. I may have been far off the mark here, and I may have been better advised to allow each project participant to select his or her own personality reflection.

I also used my relationship with and to the participants as a way to consider representation in this project. Perhaps I do not legitimately represent African American-ness or teacher education, let alone the combination of the two. I have tried to mitigate the complaints about my representation by allowing the participants to read the early draft and comment on any factual inaccuracies. However, I did not allow them to rewrite their chapters.

Crisis of Legitimation

Lincoln and Denzin (1998) refer to the move away from positivist paradigms that circumscribe legitimacy through statistical measures of validity or textual authority as the crisis of legitimation. Clearly, this volume confronts that crisis. I have drawn a small sample, and a sample of intimates at that, to make claims about the lives of African American teacher educators. I have no textual authority against which to measure my claims, because no one has seen fit previously to investigate this subject matter. So have I written legitimately about African American teacher educators? This is a question for peers to judge. I can say I have written accurately about the understanding of this group of African American teacher educators and of their experiences as African Americans and as teacher educators. They have shared stories about what it means to be in the academy, and in a bold move they have allowed themselves to be public. They chose not to hide behind pseudonyms or composite characters.

In a project like this I believe my first responsibility regarding legitimacy is to the participants. They ultimately bear the burden of being misunderstood or disliked because of how I represented them. I may only suffer from the "researcher" and "author" critiques, but my personal story is not nearly as vulnerable as those of the participants.

Although I may not have met Lincoln and Denzin's (1998) criterion of epistemological validity in this project, I do believe I have met the criterion of verisimilitude. This criterion "dispenses with the quest for validity and seeks to examine critically . . . a text's . . . ability to reproduce (simulate) and map the real" (p. 416). These are real stories of both real people. They represent both real interactions that I have had with them and their own understanding of their lives in the academy. We might quibble over whether the meanings of their experiences are shared meanings (by others who are not represented in this text), but there is no dispute over whether these are their experiences.

The Emergence of Multiple Voices

When Lincoln and Denzin (1998) speak of multiple voices, they refer to the historical exclusion of various group members (e.g., people of color, women, the poor, gays and lesbians). Clearly this is a project that embraces voices from the margins, but it would be wrong for me not to more closely examine what it means to include multiple voices and assume that I have adequately done so by virtue of the participants and the topic I have chosen.

This volume takes great liberty with its appropriation of voices from the past. I have used them to my own purposes and I have been selective in whose voices to use. I do not have the voices of a more conservative African or African American constituency, of which there are many. There is no Booker T. Washington, Edward Brooke, or Bishop Richard Allen represented among the alter egos I offer for the participants. Thus I can be legitimately seen as suppressing certain voices. This is a critique with which I must live because I am advancing a progressive project—one that is not concerned with system conservation but rather system transformation. My project pulls on voices from the past to inform our present reality.

Movement Between the Scientific and Sacred

Although Lincoln and Denzin (1998) argue that the "modernist idea of separation of religion and science overturned centuries of marriage between the two" (p. 422), a strict line between the sacred and profane has never been a part of traditional manifestations of Black culture. At a recent social gathering with some academics, one of my colleagues described attending an African American student's graduation celebration where he was shocked to see how implicated the young woman's church was in her life. He was perhaps even more surprised to hear me say that such a conjoining was a regular occurrence among Black families. The church and spirituality represent deep and important moorings for Black people in the midst of uncertainty and oppression. Although it would be essentialist and totalizing to suggest that all Black people have this religious connection, Boykin (1979) has long argued that there exist cultural dimensions among Black people that are evident across geopolitical and national boundaries. He calls one of these dimensions "spirituality" and describes it as a belief that something more transcendent is operating in one's life, for instance, that human beings are not solely in control of what happens. Science dismisses such a belief generally as superstition or in specific cases as religion and insists that there is no place for such thinking in a rational world.

However, the complexity of Black lives in the midst of overwhelming challenges rarely makes for a rational world. The ability to "make a way out of no way" and to overcome when it seems impossible is regularly and readily attributed to some force beyond individual effort—for many Black people that force is God, for others it may be referred to as "Spirit" or the ancestors. Whatever they perceive to be the source of this higher power or strength, Black people throughout history have merged the sacred and the profane as the only way to live mentally, emotionally, and psychically healthy lives.

Throughout our conversations, the project participants referred frequently to this transcendence. Perhaps if I were an outsider to the culture, I would have probed more deeply to have them articulate their beliefs. But as a participant in the culture, I found it artificial and simplistic to ask about those things that were so much of the fabric of the culture. I, too, understand the world and my life as more than material reality and my own intellectual abilities. I understand it as part of a bigger project that is integrally linked with who I am as a spiritual being.

I did not attempt to parse out the sacred from the scientific in this project. I understood the holistic nature of the participants' experiences and accepted them as such. I have tried to convey the way early experiences—both opportunities and obstacles—shaped subsequent events. I have looked at the way the personal impacts the professional rather than the more mainstream question of how the professional shapes the person (e.g., the doctor whose medical training and status shapes her identity and determines how she handles personal relationships and decisions). For me, and for the participants in this project, there is a sacredness about the work of teaching that cannot be reduced to scientific and technical principles.

Influence of Technology

Finally, Lincoln and Denzin (1998) speak to how new technologies help to make our work both easier and different. Researchers now have the ability to use electronic technologies to gather data, to analyze that information, and to interact with research participants and communities in ways that were previously unimagined. Clearly, this project benefited from my use of technology. Each interview was audiotaped. My transcriber placed each of the interviews in an electronic file that she downloaded to me. I placed the downloaded files into a qualitative data analysis software program (QSR–NVivo) to pull together analytical threads. I retrieved information about the participants via the Internet. I sent draft copies of the participants' individual chapters to them in electronic files. I used e-mail to communicate with the participants. Electronic and computer technologies made this entire project possible.

However, at a very basic level, it was the human technologies of language, relationship building, and friendship that made it the kind of project that was worth working through and bringing to completion. As I stated in Chapter 2, my attempts to interview a colleague with whom I shared no personal background yielded an adequate but less than satisfactory product. I was using the same electronic and intellectual technologies to conduct that interview. What was missing was my ability to deploy some of the human technologies that I could access with people with whom I shared some common history.

Another aspect of the project that modern technologies do not reveal is the amount of strategic rereading I had do use to merge the historical and legendary personalities I used to frame each portrait. I knew of each of the personalities (e.g., Yemajá, High John, Harriet Tubman, etc.) from childhood tales and from reading over a lifetime. However, I had not thought about how their examples could serve as templates for the work people are trying to do today. This strategy may seem foreign in educational research circles, but most people (regardless of race, ethnicity, and culture) can point to people whose lives served as a positive and motivating model for how they wanted to live their lives. Former President Bill Clinton regularly spoke of the influence John F. Kennedy had on his life course. Many people reference the role of parents and family members in helping to shape and guide the direction their lives took. What I attempted to do was to reach back and select a person whose larger-than-life contributions and presence served as a credible parallel to the character and influence of the modern-day personalities I tried to represent. One might argue that I tried to employ a cultural technology.

By cultural technology I mean that I used the language, social competencies, trust, reciprocity, and shared understandings with the participants to ensure clear and open communication to produce this volume. Our past relationships made it unlikely that they would withhold information or deceive me in the process. Nor would I be likely to try to construct them in unflattering or impersonal ways. Unlike my late father who took great pride in "deceiving" the government by lying on the U.S. Census forms, I designed my cultural technology to allow for a high degree of transparency. Not only do I know the participants but I also shared the sort of relationships with them that are bound to continue. We will be in each other's lives beyond the production of this text. In some ways this project represents a kind of postmodern turn in that there is text that precedes this volume (our previous relationships) and text that succeeds this volume (our ongoing and future relationships) that I, as researcher, have and will live out. Perhaps this is the fifth moment to which Lincoln and Denzin (1998) allude.

CODA

As much as scholars desire to complete a project, there is something about this completion that is deeply painful. For the past year I have been able to regularly count on sifting through interview transcripts and biographies to craft these portraits of my colleagues. I have been able to talk about "my work" with other colleagues. I have searched archives for obscure biographical references and have relished the idea of pulling together comparisons and new ways to think about my colleagues and their work.

Like a portraitist, I have lovingly taken the canvas cover off the easel each day and done touch-up work. I have tried painting with both bold strokes and fine shadings. I have mixed my oils and come up with new colors. My "subjects" have sat patiently before me and bared their souls for my flawed eyes and limited talents to create a thing of beauty. Most surprising about this project is the complete trust the participants placed in my ability to render them in the best light with their best features made prominent.

As long as I was continuing to work on this project, I could bask in the belief that I was doing right by the participants. But as I conclude the work, I am terrified about how they might feel about the finished project. I am less concerned about the critical response—for every accolade I have received, I have always had a dozen negative criticisms. That is the nature of life in the academy; indeed, in this business, if no one is criticizing your work, it probably means that no one is reading it.

This work is a different kind of work for me. It is as close to both voyeurism and navel gazing as I have ever come. I spent time looking into the personal and professional lives of some dear colleagues, and I insinuated myself into not only their lives but also the stories I have told about them. I feel vindicated in my choices here because of my beliefs (and research) about pedagogy. I know that pedagogy is deeply personal work that can be successful only if we harness our human technologies to interact and engage with students, colleagues, and community members on very intimate and personal levels.

The work of preparing teachers for an incredibly diverse school population requires the kind of insights that the teacher educators in this volume have shared. It requires our teacher education institutions and our majority-group-member colleagues to regard us as more than tokens and oddities in the academy. I have tried to detail the ways in which our work cries out for expanded spaces and possibilities. And as I reluctantly draw this volume to a close, I am heartened by the idea that we can do important multicultural, antiracist, feminist, democratic work that moves us all beyond the Big House.

NOTES

1. I know I am omitting someone and apologize in advance for my sketchy memory.

2. My daughter is a college freshman at this writing.

3. Lincoln and Denzin (1998) refer to the fifth moment as the present. While many researchers are concerned with the "sixth moment" or the future, these authors remind us that "Writing in the present is always dangerous, a biased project conditioned by distorted readings of the past and utopian hopes for the future" (p. 407) .

References

American Association of Colleges for Teacher Education. (1994). *Briefing books.* Washington, DC: Author.

Anderegg, D. (2003). *Worried all the time: Overparenting in an age of anxiety.* New York: The Free Press.

Asante, M. K. (1987). *The Afrocentric idea.* Philadelphia: Temple University Press.

Banks, C. A. M. (1977, April). A content analysis of the treatment of Black Americans on television. *Social Education, 41,* 336–340.

Banks, C. A. M. (1995). Intellectual leadership and the influence of early African American scholars on multicultural education. *Educational Policy, 9*(3), 260–280.

Banks, C. A. M. (2004). *Improving multicultural education: Lessons from the intergroup education movement.* New York: Teachers College Press.

Banks, J. A. (Ed.). (1996). *Multicultural education, transformative knowledge, and action: Historical and contemporary perspectives.* New York: Teachers College Press.

Banks, J. A. (2004). Multicultural education: Historical development, dimensions, and practice. In J. A. Banks & C. A. M. Banks (Eds.), *Handbook of research on multicultural education* (2nd ed.). San Francisco: Jossey-Bass.

Banks, J. A., & Banks, C. A. M. (Eds.). (2004). *Handbook of research on multicultural education* (2nd ed.). San Francisco: Josey-Bass.

Bateson, M. C. (1989). *Composing a life.* New York: Atlantic Monthly Press.

Bell, D. (1987). *And we are not saved: The elusive quest for racial justice.* New York: Basic Books.

Bell, D. (1992). *Faces at the bottom of the well.* New York: Basic Books.

Bell, D. (2002). *Ethical ambition.* New York: Bloomsbury.

Boykin, A. W. (1979). Psychological/behavioral verve: Some theoretical explorations and empirical manifestations. In A. W. Boykin, A. W. Franklin, J. Yates (Eds.), *Research directions of Black psychologists* (pp. 351–367). New York: Russell Sage Foundation.

Bruner, E. M. (1993). Introduction: The ethnographic self and the personal self. In P. Benson (Ed.), *Anthropology and literature* (pp. 1–26). Urbana: University of Illinois Press.

Clark, R. (1984). *Family life and school achievement: Why poor Black children succeed or fail.* Chicago: University of Chicago Press.

CNN.com. (2002, October 16). Belafonte won't back down from Powell slave reference [Radio interview]. Retrieved from www.cnn.com/2002/US/10/15/belafonte.powell

Collins, P. H. (1991). *Black feminist thought.* New York: Routledge.

Collins, P. H. (1998). *Fighting words: Black women and the search for justice.* Minneapolis: University of Minnesota Press.

Cooper, A. J. (1988). *A voice from the south.* New York: Oxford University Press. (Original work published 1892)

Crane, B. (1985). *Charlotte Forten's mission: Experiment in freedom* [Video recording]. Monterey, CA: Monterey Video.

Crenshaw, K. (1988). Race, reform, and retrenchment: Transformation and legitimation in antidiscrimination law. *Harvard Law Review, 101,* 1331–1387.

De la luz Reyes, M., & Halcón, J. (1988). Racism in academia: The old wolf revisited. *Harvard Educational Review, 58*(3), 299–314.

Delgado, R. (Ed.). (1995). *Critical race theory: The cutting edge.* Philadelphia: Temple University Press.

Delpit, L. (1986). Skills and other dilemmas of a progressive Black educator. *Harvard Educational Review, 56*(4), 379–385.

Delpit, L. (1988). The silenced dialogue: Power and pedagogy in educating other people's children. *Harvard Educational Review, 58*(3), 280–298.

Delpit, L. (1995). *Other people's children: Cultural conflict in the classroom.* New York: The Free Press.

Demaratus, D. (2002). *The force of a feather: The search for a lost story of slavery and freedom.* Salt Lake City: University of Utah Press.

Dews, C. L. B., & Law, C. L. L. (Eds.). (1995). *This fine place so far from home: Voices of academicians from the working class.* Philadelphia: Temple University Press.

Drake, S. C., & Cayton, H. (1993). *Black metropolis.* Chicago: University of Chicago Press. (Original work published 1945)

DuBois, W. E. B. (1953). *The souls of Black folks.* New York: Fawcett. (Original work published 1903)

Ducharme, E. (1993). *The lives of teacher educators.* New York: Teachers College Press.

Ducharme, E., & Agne, R. (1989). Professors of education: Uneasy residents of academe. In R. Wisniewski & E. Ducharme (Eds.), *The profession of teaching: An inquiry* (pp. 67–86). Albany: State University of New York Press.

Ducharme, E., & Kluender, M. (1990). The RATE study: The faculty. *Journal of Teacher Education, 41*(4), 45–49.

Eakin, S., & Logsdon, J. (Eds.). (1968). *Twelve years as a slave by Solomon Northrup.* Baton Rouge: Louisiana State Press.

Featherstone, J. (1989). To make the wounded whole. *Harvard Educational Review, 59,* 367–378.

Federal Writers' Project. (n. d.) Retrieved March 11, 2002, from http://memory.loc.gov/amem/snbtml/snhome.html

Foner, E. (Ed.). (1971). *Nat Turner.* Englewood Cliffs, NJ: Prentice Hall.

Forten, C. (1864, May). Life on the Sea Islands. *Atlantic Monthly, 13,* 587–596.

Foster, M. (1989). It's cookin' now: A performance analysis of the speech events of a Black teacher in an urban community college. *Linguistics in Society, 18,* 1–29.

Foster, M. (1997). *Black teachers on teaching.* New York: The New Press.

Franklin, J. H. (1988). *From slavery to freedom* (6th ed.) New York: Alfred A. Knopf.

Frierson, H. (1990). The situation of Black educational researchers: Continuation of a crisis. *Educational Researcher, 19*(2), 12–17.

Fuller, F., & Brown, O. (1975). Becoming a teacher. In K. Ryan (Ed.), *Teacher education,* 74th Yearbook of the National Society for the Study of Education (Pt. 2, pp. 25–52). Chicago: University of Chicago Press.

Gates, H. L. (1997, April 4). *The achievement of the Norton Anthology of African American Literature.* Paper presented at conference on Canonizing African American Literature: Black anthologies in America 1843–1996, University of Wisconsin, Madison, WI.

Gay, G. (1985). Implications of selected models of ethnic identity development for educators. *The Journal of Negro Education, 54*(1), 43–55.

Gay, G. (2000). *Culturally responsive teaching: Theory, research, and practice.* New York: Teachers College Press.

Gay, G. (2004). Curriculum theory and multicultural education. In J. A. Banks & C. A. M. Banks (Eds.), *Handbook of research on multicultural education* (2nd ed., pp. 30–49). San Francisco: Jossey-Bass.

Gay, G., & Baber, W. (Eds.) (1987). *Expressively Black: The cultural basis of ethnic identity.* New York: Praeger.

Giddings, P. (1984). *When and where I enter: The impact of Black women on race and sex in America.* New York: William Morrow.

Grant, C. A., & Sleeter, C. E. (2003). *Turning on learning* (3rd ed.). New York: J. W. Wiley.

Grundy, S., & Hatton, E. (1998). Teacher educators, student teachers and biographical influences: Implications for teacher education. *Asia-Pacific Journal of Teacher Education, 26*(2), 121–137.

Haberman, M. (1995). *Star teachers of children in poverty.* West Lafayette, IN: Kappa Delta Pi.

Irvine, J. J. (1990). *Black students and school failure: Personnel, practices, and prescriptions.* Westport, CT: Greenwood Press.

Kaplan, C. (Ed.). (2001). *Zora Neale Hurston: Every tongue got to confess: Negro folk-tales from the gulf states.* New York: HarperCollins.

Karen, D. (1990). Toward a political-organizational model of gatekeeping: The case of elite colleges. *Sociology of Education, 63*(4), 227–240.

Karenga, R. (2000). Black Religion: The African model. In L. G. Murphy (Ed.), *Down by the riverside: Readings in African American religion* (pp. 41–48). New York: New York University Press.

Kern-Foxworthy, M. (1994). *Aunt Jemima, Uncle Ben and Rastus: Blacks in advertising yesterday, today and tomorrow.* New York: Praeger.

King, J. E. (1991). Dysconscious racism: Ideology, identity, and the miseducation of teachers. *The Journal of Negro Education, 60,* 133–146.

King, J. E. (1992). Diaspora literacy and consciousness in the struggle against mis-education in the Black community. *The Journal of Negro Education, 61,* 317–340.

King, J. E. (1995). Culture centered knowledge: Black studies, curriculum transformation, and social action. In J. A. Banks & C. A. M. Banks (Eds.), *Handbook of research in multicultural education* (pp. 265–290). New York: Macmillan.

King, J. E., & Mitchell, C. (1995). *Black mothers to sons: Juxtaposing African American literature with social practice.* New York: Peter Lang. (Original work published 1990)

Ladson-Billings, G. (1994). *The dreamkeepers: Successful teachers of African American children.* San Francisco: Jossey Bass.

Ladson-Billings, G. (1996). Silences as weapons: Challenges of a Black professor teaching White students. *Theory Into Practice, 35*(2), 79–85.

Ladson-Billings, G. (2000, May). *National Partnership on Education and Accountability in Teaching.* Final Report.

Ladson-Billings, G. (2002). *Beyond the Big House: African American teacher educators' perspectives on teacher education.* Paper presented at the Annual Meeting of the American Educational Research Association, New Orleans, LA.

Ladson-Billings, G. (2003). *Pay no attention to the person behind the curtain: The limits of teacher education in preparing teachers for diversity.* Paper presented at the annual meeting of the American Educational Research Association, Chicago, IL.

Ladson-Billings, G., & Tate, W. F. (1995). Toward a critical race theory of education. *Teachers College Record, 97*(1), 47–68.

Law, C. L. (1995). Introduction. In C. L. B. Dews & C. L. Law (Eds.), *This fine place so far from home* (pp. 1–10). Philadelphia: Temple University Press.

Lawrence-Lightfoot, S., & Davis, J. (1997). *The art and science of portraiture.* San Francisco: Jossey-Bass.

Lemert, C. (1998). Anna Julia Cooper: The colored woman's office. In C. Lemertand & E. Bhan (Eds.), *The voice of Anna Julia Cooper* (pp. 1–43). Lanham, MD: Rowman & Littlefield.

Lemert, C., & Bhan, E. (Eds.). (1998). *The voice of Anna Julia Cooper.* Lanham, MD: Rowman & Littlefield.

Lerner, G. (Ed.). (1972). *Black women in White America: A documentary history.* New York: Pantheon Books.

Lincoln, Y., & Denzin, N. (1998). The fifth moment. In N. Denzin & Y. Lincoln, *The landscape of qualitative research: Theories and issues* (pp. 407–429). Thousand Oaks, CA: Sage.

Lorde, A. (1981). The master's tools will never dismantle the master's house. In C. Moraga & G. Anzaldua (Eds.), *This bridge called my back: Writings by radical women of color* (pp. 98–101). New York: Kitchen Table: Women of Color.

Lubrano, A. (2003). *Limbo: Blue collar roots, white collar dreams.* New York: John Wiley & Sons.

Malcolm X. (1965, February 4). *The house Negro and the field Negro* [Speech]. Brown Chapel AME Church, Selma, AL.

Malvasi, M. G. (2003, February 12). Trickster tales. Retrieved October 29, 2003, from www.suite101.com/article.cfm/3679/98827

Manring, M. (1998). *Slave in a box: The strange career of Aunt Jemima.* Charlottesville: University of Virginia Press.

Moll, L. C. (1992). Funds of knowledge: Using a qualitative approach to connect homes and classrooms. *Theory into Practice, 31*(2), 132–141.

Murphy, L. G. (Ed.). (2000). *Down by the riverside: Readings in African American religion.* New York: New York University Press.

National Commission on Teaching and America's Future. (1996). *What matters most: Teaching and America's future.* New York: Author.

Nobles, A. W. (1973). Psychological research and the Black self-concept: A critical review. *Journal of Social Issues, 29,* 11–31.

Padilla, A. (1994). Ethnic minority scholars, research, and mentoring: Current and future issues. *Educational Researcher, 23*(4), 24–27.

Paseornek, M. (Producer), & Forester, M. (Director). (2001). *Monster's ball* [Motion picture]. United States: Lion's Gate Films.

Quarles, B. (1964). *The Negro in the making of America.* New York: Collier Books.

Quarles, B. (1989). *The Negro in the civil war.* New York: Da Capo Press. (Original work published 1953)

Richards, D. (1985). The implications of African-American spirituality. In M. K. Asante & K. W. Asante (Eds.), *African culture: The rhythms of unity* (pp. 207–231). Westport, CT: Greenwood Press.

Saar, B. (1972). The liberation of Aunt Jemima [Art exhibit]. *University Art Museum and Pacific Film Archive.* Berkeley: University of California.

Sawyer, M. R. (2000). Sources of Black denominationalism. In L. G. Murphy (Ed.), *Down by the riverside: Readings in African American religion* (pp. 59–67). New York: New York University Press.

Shah, I. (1971). *The wisdom of the idiots.* New York: E. P. Dutton.

Shea, C. (1992, August 5). California Supreme Court upholds big award in tenure bias case. *The Chronicle of Higher Education,* p. A12.

Sleeter, C. (2001). Preparing teachers for culturally diverse schools: Research and the overwhelming presence of Whiteness. *Journal of Teacher Education, 52*(2), 94–106.

Sleeter, C. E., & Grant, C. A. (1987). An analysis of multicultural education in the U.S.A. *Harvard Educational Review, 57,* 421–444.

Sleeter, C. E., & Grant, C. A. (2003). *Making choices for multicultural education: Five approaches to race, class, and gender* (4th ed.). New York: J. W. Wiley.

Tate, W. F. (1997). Critical race theory and education: History, theory and implications. *Review of Research in Education* (vol. 22, pp. 191–243). Washington, DC: American Educational Research Association.

Tate, W. F., Ladson-Billings, G., & Grant, C. A. (1993). The Brown decision revisited: Mathematizing social problems. *Educational Policy, 7,* 255–275.

Timeline. (n. d.). Harriet Tubman, 1819–1913. Retrieved November 25, 2003, from www.math.buffalo.edu/~sww/0history/hwny-tubman.html

Tokarczyk, M. M., & Fay, E. (Eds.). (1993). *Working class women in the academy: Laborers in the knowledge factory*. Amherst: University of Massachusetts Press.

Viadero, D. (1996, March 13). Lisa Delpit says teachers must value students' cultural strengths. *Education Week*. Retrieved April 23, 2004, from www.edweek.org/ewstory.cfm?slug=delpit.h15&keywords=Lisa%20Delpit

Wiencek, H. (2003). *An imperfect god: George Washington, his slaves and the creation of America*. New York: Farrar, Straus, and Giroux.

Wills, G. (2003). *Negro president: Jefferson and the slave power*. Boston: Houghton Mifflin.

Woodson, C. G. (1990). *The mis-education of the Negro*. Trenton, NJ: Africa World Press. (Original work published 1933)

Wynter, S. (1992). *Do not call us 'negros': How multicultural textbooks perpetuate racism*. San Francisco: Aspire Books.

Zimpher, N., & Sherrill, J. (1996). Professors, teachers, and leaders in schools, colleges, and departments of education. In J. Sikula (Ed.), *Handbook of research on teacher education* (pp. 279–305). New York: Macmillan.

Index

About the Author

Gloria Ladson-Billings is the Kellner Family Professor of Urban Education in the Department of Curriculum and Instruction at the University of Wisconsin-Madison, and the 2005 president of the American Educational Research Association. Ladson-Billings's research examines the pedagogical practices of teachers who are successful with African American students. She also investigates Critical Race Theory applications to education. She is the author of the critically acclaimed book *The Dreamkeepers: Successful Teachers of African American Children, Crossing Over to Canaan: The Journey of New Teachers in Diverse Classrooms*, and many journal articles and book chapters. She is the former editor of the *American Educational Research Journal* and a member of several editorial boards.

Gloria Ladson-Billings's work has won numerous scholarly awards, including the H. I. Romnes faculty fellowship, the Spencer Post-Doctoral Fellowship, and the Palmer O. Johnson Outstanding research award. In 2002 she was awarded an honorary doctorate from Umeå University in Umeå, Sweden, and in 2003–2004 was a fellow at the Center for Advanced Study in the Behavioral Sciences at Stanford University. She is the 2004 recipient of the George and Louise Spindler Award for ongoing contributions in educational anthropology, given by the Council on Anthropology & Education of the American Anthropological Association. Gloria lives in Madison, Wisconsin, with her husband, Charles, and daughter, Jessica.